Windows® XP

© Haynes Publishing 2003
Reprinted 2004

Published by: Haynes Publishing
Sparkford, Yeovil, Somerset BA22 7JJ, UK
Tel: 01963 442030 Fax: 01963 440001
Int. tel: +44 1963 442030 Fax: +44 1963 440001
E-mail: sales@haynes.co.uk
Web site: www.haynes.co.uk

British Library Cataloguing in Publication Data:
A catalogue record for this book is available from the British Library

ISBN 1 84425 033 4

Printed in Britain by J. H. Haynes & Co. Ltd., Sparkford

Windows® XP

XP

The survival manual

Kyle MacRae

Contents

Introduction

Imagine, if you will, a Windows user not a million miles removed from this page making a semi-enforced upgrade to Windows XP while on deadline one busy afternoon in early 2002. Let us say that he spent all of, oh, three minutes or so taking in the landscape before plunging on with his work. Let us further suppose that for the next few weeks he was never quite sure why he sometimes saw thumbnails of his images in Windows Explorer and sometimes did not, was never wholly certain why his My Documents folder had upped sticks nor where it now lived, and once managed to lock himself out of his own computer.

If there is a lesson to be learned from this – and with the benefit of hindsight our subject would certainly concur – it is that a little time spent getting to grips with Windows XP at the outset means a much more rewarding experience thereafter. Our goal here is to help you hit the ground running and make a painless, hopefully rewarding, transition from an earlier version of Windows to Windows XP.

Ins and outs

Any guide that deals with a subject as vast as Windows is necessarily selective. This, then, is a personal look at XP, an exercise in pruning, with a focus on the areas and features that we have found most important and productive.

In particular, we do not touch upon XP's multimedia capabilities. This may strike you as odd: after all, XP is explicitly designed to appeal to people who work with images, music files and video. The Windows Media Player application is, or at least seems to be, central to the whole shebang yet we do not mention it once. Nor does Windows Movie Maker, a basic but effective video editor for home-movie enthusiasts, merit so much as a mention. Why?

Partly for reasons of space, to be honest, but mainly because such applications are strictly non-essential. A multi-functional multimedia player bundled with Windows may be a bonus but it is not integral to the operation system: you can get along without it, and you can certainly get some excellent third-party alternatives. In some cases, notably Windows XP's firewall, its built-in CD-burning capability and the MS Backup utility, third-party applications can make a better fist of the task in hand. We would therefore encourage you to explore everything XP has to offer but then continue to explore beyond its confines. Here we concentrate on Windows XP the operating system, not Windows XP the kitchen sink.

The one major exception to this is with Windows Messenger, which we look at in some detail in Part Seven. Instant messaging per se is not dependent upon a computer's operating system and there are plenty of alternative services to choose from. Windows Messenger does, however, offer a straightforward gateway to powerful features like videoconferencing and Application Sharing, and we feel it merits special inclusion here.

Survive or succumb

From whichever direction you come to Windows XP, be you a home user upgrading from Windows 98 or Millennium Edition, a business user reluctantly relinquishing the stability of Windows 2000, or a complete newcomer to computing, there is no escaping the fact that XP fronts a bold, colourful and rather brash face to the world while offering a significantly different hands-on experience to that of its predecessors. Our approach here is to assume that you are on the verge of making the switch to XP or have recently done so and could use a roadmap around this strange new territory on your desktop. Finding familiar Windows elements, understanding how they work in an unfamiliar world and uncovering new features and approaches are all essential steps towards surviving your Windows eXPerience.

Conventions used in this book

Single click on the left mouse button

Double-click on the left mouse button

Single click on the right mouse button

Check or uncheck this option by clicking the left mouse button

Type the following text on your keyboard

Wherever possible, we illustrate actions with screenshots and describe them in the text.

Screen examples

Mouse instructions

Keyboard instructions

Text instructions

④ New Folder icon
Rename this folder
Home Finances [Enter]

This step only applies if Step 3 goes wrong and you did-n't manage to rename the folder while 'New Folder' was highlighted. Select New Folder by clicking its icon once. Now look in the left window pane and you'll see an option to Rename this folder. Click this and once again the folder's title becomes highlighted. Now just type in the new name and press the Enter key. Any folder can be renamed in this manner.

⑤ Home Finances icon
Make a new folder
Bank Correspondence [Enter]

... the example discussed above, we now want to ... Home Finances called Bank

1

WINDOWS XP

PART 1 Installing Windows XP

PART **1** Why Windows XP?

For the avoidance of any possible doubt, Windows XP is the latest in a line of operating systems for personal computers developed and marketed by Microsoft. XP actually evolved from the business-minded Windows NT and 2000 product ranges but it retains little of their austerity and complexity. Indeed, on the surface it has all the feel and flavour of a funky family-friendly operating system, more akin to Windows 95, 98 or Millennium Edition. It is only when you look under the skin – a bright blue skin called Luna, incidentally – that you discover XP's true pedigree.

Windows 2000 was long the business user's operating system of choice: not ideal for games-playing but commendably crash-proof. Windows XP now bridges the domestic and business markets.

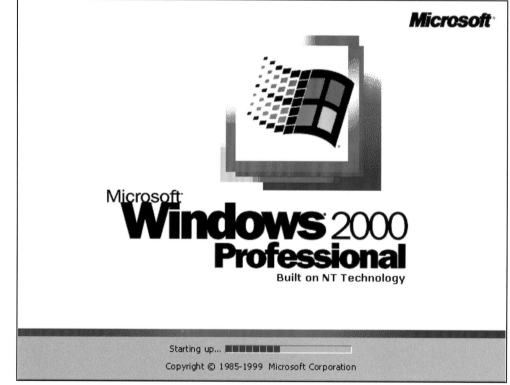

Of course, most computer users have neither the need nor the desire to look under the skin and we have no intention of blathering on earnestly about kernels and architecture here. So let us put our cards on the table right at the outset: it is our considered opinion that Windows XP is the 'best' operating system choice for computers in business and the home. Our criteria for saying so is fourfold: a) XP is stable; b) XP is easy to use; c) XP is more likely to support the digital cameras, MP3 players, PDAs, memory card readers and other devices you want to hook up to your hardware today; and d) XP is more likely to support the application software you want to run.

Windows remains overwhelmingly the most popular operating system for personal computers. XP is its latest incarnation.

But perhaps more relevant than any of that is the stark reality that, in an operating system marketplace devoid of meaningful competition, you will probably end up using XP sooner or later regardless. 'Why Windows XP?' is therefore something of a redundant question: short of buying a Mac or taking a crash-course in Linux, Windows XP is just the way it is right now. So, given that you may have to like it or lump it, learning how to work with rather than against XP is, we suggest, the more profitable path – and something we hope to help you with here.

QUICK Q&A

I used to run out of memory with Windows Me, even when I closed running programs. Will this still happen with XP?
No. Like Windows 2000 before it, Windows XP manages memory more efficiently and ensures that programs release RAM back to the general pool as soon as possible. This means that you no longer have to periodically reboot just to keep the system running.

Totals		Physical Memory (K)	
Handles	7711	Total	1048048
Threads	404	Available	727352
Processes	39	System Cache	288848

Commit Charge (K)		Kernel Memory (K)	
Total	177896	Total	69568
Limit	1735224	Paged	29236
Peak	194072	Nonpaged	40332

All for one…

For Microsoft, pulling off the trick of combining its business and domestic operating systems into a single product was always going to be a gamble that risked alienating both user camps. True, there are actually two flavours of XP – Home Edition and Professional – but the differences between them are far less significant than between, say, Windows 98 and Windows 2000. Whether Microsoft has ultimately succeeded is moot but more a matter of taste and opinion than of hard fact. We will say this, though: because XP was designed for both the beginner and the seasoned Windows user, it strikes a sometimes uneasy balance between instant ease of use and intrusive hand-holding. Recurring popup bubbles, animated search tools and the many ways in which Windows tries to second-guess your next move may appeal to your computer-as-friend sensibilities – or may drive you to distraction.

The Home Edition and Professional versions of Windows XP are essentially the same product at heart. The latter has a few extra features – and a correspondingly higher price tag.

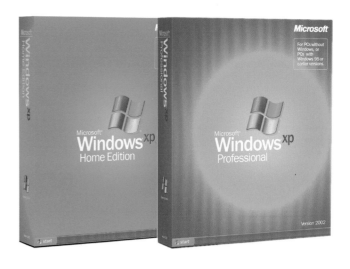

PART 1 Upgrading seamlessly

If you have just bought a new computer with Windows XP pre-installed, you may want to skip right on ahead to something more interesting. But if you're heading for the superstore this very afternoon, intent on grabbing a copy of XP for your existing system, this section is for you. Upgrading may be a fact of computing life but it is seldom something to undertake casually or without forethought and planning. This is particularly true where the operating system is concerned. It may just be the means to an end – that end being doing useful stuff with your computer – but it impacts upon the way you work at every level.

Home Edition or Professional?

At one level, both the Home Edition and Professional versions of Windows XP offer the same welcome improvements over earlier releases of Windows: greater stability and reliability, relative simplicity and increased flexibility. Under the surface, they are all-but identical. This contrasts favourably with the consumer-flavoured Windows Me and business-oriented Windows 2000 duopoly where, despite sharing a broadly similar interface, the first was a flaky upgrade from Windows 98 while the second was built around an altogether different and more stable core. XP takes its cue and its kernel from Windows 2000.

Why, then, would you be tempted by the more expensive Professional release over Home Edition? Here are the key additional features with Professional:

Feature	Purpose
Remote Desktop	Log in to your computer remotely across the internet while you travel
File encryption	Secure sensitive files with strong encryption (see p116)
Access controls	Fine-tune the ways in which different users may access specific files and folders (see p106). Home Edition takes a blunderbuss approach to privacy, as we shall see.
Domain participation	The computer can join and be managed by a corporate domain-based network, with support for user roaming. Home Edition supports only workgroup-based networks.
Offline Files	A kind of supercharged Briefcase-style feature where you work on cached copies of network files on the road and synch folders when you return

Windows XP Professional offers greater scope and security for networks and mobile workers.

In short, if additional security or (very) advanced networking are important to you, consider paying the premium for Professional.

Full version or upgrade?

As you may have noticed while perusing the shelves, both versions of Windows XP come in two varieties: Upgrade and Full. Upgrade products are considerably cheaper but you must be a Windows user to qualify. It's a kind of loyalty bonus, if you will. Ostensibly, the upgrade qualification path is this:

Upgrade from...	
Windows XP Home Edition	Windows 98 Windows 98SE (Second Edition) Windows Me (Millennium Edition)
Windows XP Professional	Windows 98 Windows 98SE (Second Edition) Windows Me (Millennium Edition) Windows NT Workstation 4.0 Windows 2000 Professional Windows XP Home Edition

However, this is not quite as straightforward as it sounds. You might assume that an Upgrade CD-ROM will only work when there is a current, active version of Windows on your computer to upgrade, but in fact this is not the case. The clue is hidden in this phrase on the side of the box:

'The enclosed program will search your hard disk and/or CD to confirm your eligibility for this upgrade'.

What this means in practice is that it is sufficient to produce a qualifying Windows CD-ROM on demand. During installation, the Windows XP Setup program looks for a copy of Windows on the hard disk. If it finds one, as it would if you install XP over the top of Windows 98, for example, all well and good; if it doesn't, as would be the case in a clean installation on a new hard disk, Setup halts and demands evidence that you have the right to use an Upgrade CD-ROM. At this point, you merely need to pop a qualifying Windows CD-ROM in the drive, whereupon Setup continues.

An upgrade version of Windows XP is all you need if you own a qualifying version of Windows.

The upshot is that it is perfectly possible to perform a clean installation with an Upgrade copy of Windows XP so long as you have an old copy of Windows to hand – so dig out your old discs and save yourself a packet. Windows 95 or 3.1 users are unfortunately out of luck; you must stump up for the Full version.

Preliminary checks

One of the key differences between Windows XP and earlier versions of Windows, with the partial exception of Windows 2000, is that XP is very particular about what hardware and software it will and will not work with (i.e. support). It is possible to install Windows XP and suddenly find that, for instance, you can no longer use your printer. Long-term, this is arguably a good thing: by insisting that hardware meets stringent compatibility guidelines, Windows protects itself from clashes and crashes. We say 'arguably' because it would be better if everything 'just worked' always and forever, but that is not the way of things in this world.

If a hardware device is incompatible with Windows XP, a driver update is usually all that is required. By now, most manufacturers have either released Windows XP drivers or made it plain that they have no intention of doing so, which effectively renders a host of older but still serviceable hardware redundant. In some cases, a Windows 2000 driver will suffice; in others, you may have no option but to replace your hardware. The same consideration applies to unsupported software.

However, these considerations only apply if, when you upgrade to Windows XP, you ditch your current version of Windows in the process i.e. overwrite it with XP. We will shortly consider some baby-plus-bath water ways to avoid this dilemma.

Checking your kit

Meanwhile, there are four things you can do upfront to minimise any unfavourable consequences of upgrading to Windows XP.

- First, pay a visit to the Windows Catalog website: www.microsoft.com/windows/catalog. Here you can look up your existing hardware devices and software programs and establish whether they were 'designed for' Windows XP (guaranteed to work) or 'compatible with' Windows XP (should work okay). If some of your devices or programs are not listed, they may not have been submitted to Microsoft for explicit XP-approval. A Microsoft-issued 'designed for' or 'compatible with' XP logo is reassuring but not strictly essential i.e. your hardware and software may work regardless. The next step is to visit the manufacturer or developer's website. Look in the Support section and see whether there are XP drivers, patches or updates available for download.

Check your hardware for XP-compatibility with Windows Catalog.

- Alternatively, download a copy of the Windows XP Upgrade Advisor: www.microsoft.com/windowsxp/pro/howtobuy/ upgrading/advisor.asp. This utility checks your computer for compatibility. The only snag – and it's a serious one – is the size of the Advisor program: at over 30MB, it could take the best part of two hours to download over a dialup (modem) connection. When you have the UpgAdv.exe file saved to your computer, run the program. If your computer is connected to the internet, or can be connected, allow it to search Microsoft's site for updated files. Upgrade Advisor then scans your system for compatibility and flags up potential problems in a report.

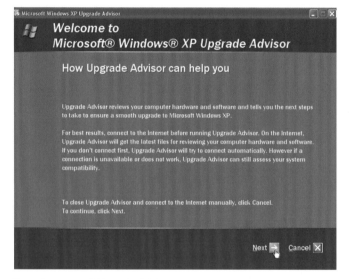

There is a copy of Upgrade Advisor on the XP installation CD.

- If you already have a Windows XP CD-ROM in your possession, you'll find a version of Upgrade Advisor on the disc. This kicks in automatically when you begin an installation procedure but can also be run independently in advance. Pop the CD-ROM in the drive and select Check System Compatibility from the welcome menu. In the next screen, click Check My System automatically and wait for the report. If Upgrade Advisor finds a problem device or program, and assuming that you can locate an XP driver or patch for it, we suggest that you download any updates now and save them to floppy or CD-R media. Uninstall the troublesome device or program before upgrading to XP. Later, when all else is well, reinstall it and use the XP-compliant driver or apply the patch.

Get an upfront low-down on trouble ahead with Upgrade Advisor.

- Finally, whichever installation method you plump for, make a backup copy of your important files now. Also make sure that you still have your old program installation CD-ROMs to hand. There's nothing worse than waving a final goodbye to your familiar Windows setup only to discover yourself unable to reinstall your favourite word processor or image editor.

Program Compatibility mode

Should you ever find that so-called legacy software (i.e. anything that's a few years old) fails to work properly after you've installed Windows XP, especially computer games, all is not quite lost. Right-click the icon that normally launches the program – you can use the Start menu or any shortcut that points at the executable file – and open the Compatibility tab. Check the Compatibility mode box and select your previous operating system (or the version of Windows for which the program was originally designed). Results are not guaranteed but a little behind-the-scenes trickery masks some of XP's newer features and might just coax your program or game back into action.

QuickTime Player Properties

General | Shortcut | Compatibility

If you have problems with this program and it worked correctly on an earlier version of Windows, select the compatibility mode that matches that earlier version.

Compatibility mode

☑ Run this program in compatibility mode for:

Windows 98 / Windows Me

Windows 95
Windows 98 / Windows Me
Windows NT 4.0 (Service Pack 5)
Windows 2000
☐ Run in 256 colors

☐ Run in 640 x 480 screen resolution

☐ Disable visual themes

Input settings
☐ Turn off advanced text services for this program

Learn more about program compatibility.

OK | Cancel | Apply

Compatibility mode lets you run older software on Windows XP.

Minimum requirements

Before installing Windows XP, be sure that your hardware is up to spec. The recommended system requirements, as decreed by Microsoft, are as follows:

- 300MHz processor
- 128MB RAM
- 1.5GB free hard disk space

All three requirements are rather optimistic but RAM is by far the most important. Windows XP will actually run – well, limp – with a mere 64MB of onboard memory but 256MB is, in our view, a more realistic figure. There is little point 'upgrading' your operating system if the net result is a slower computer.

Transfer files and settings

Chances are you have your computer set up more or less as you like it, and the prospect of having to reconfigure everything from scratch under Windows XP is daunting. Don't underestimate the task: for starters, you probably have a gargantuan list of bookmarked internet sites to preserve. And then there are program tweaks that took time to get right, customised toolbars, file associations, a custom dictionary in your word processor, personal mouse, keyboard and display preferences, perhaps a Desktop theme, program shortcuts, internet and home network settings, hundreds of saved e-mails, a nested hierarchy of folders within My Documents... well, the list just goes on and on. The thought of having to reconfigure all this stuff is enough to put anybody off an upgrade.

A welcome Windows wizard

Thankfully, Windows XP includes a utility that makes light work of shifting settings from hither to thither. Although it is primarily designed for moving information from one computer to another, it comes in equally handy when upgrading from an older version of Windows to XP on the same system.

In this worked example, we will run the Files and Settings Transfer Wizard directly from the Windows XP installation CD-ROM on a PC running Windows Me. Three points to note:

- The wizard saves all files and settings that you specify within a single file. This file may be a few Megabytes or several Gigabytes in size, depending upon the files and folders you select for inclusion. It is important to make a backup copy of this file before proceeding with an XP upgrade in case it gets lost or corrupted in the process. Either keep it within manageable proportions – under 700MB if you have a recordable CD drive, for instance – or transfer it to another computer through a network connection. We suggest that you let the wizard focus on system and program settings and manually back up your important files and folders – i.e. everything in the My Documents folder, or wherever else you keep your data – in a separate operation. These files can be easily restored later.

Back up your files and folders separately to keep the wizard's file size to a minimum.

An oversized Files and Settings Wizard file can be awkward to copy. At 176MB, this one will comfortably fit on a CD-R disc.

- When performing an over-the-top upgrade – that is, simply upgrading your current version of Windows to Windows XP, as discussed in detail on p20–24 – most non-system files and settings will (well, should) be preserved intact. There is thus no absolute necessity to use the Files and Settings Transfer Wizard in such a scenario, but we still recommend doing so just in case the installation procedure goes awry. Re-configuring Windows from scratch is a right royal pain.

- If you already have multiple users set up on your computer – i.e. different people can log on with their own passwords – you must run the Files and Settings Transfer Wizard separately for each user. Save the resultant files separately. When XP is up and running, log on as each user in turn and restore their respective files and settings from the appropriate file.

1

- *Perform additional tasks*
- *Transfer files and settings*

Place the Windows XP disc in your CD or DVD drive and wait for the Welcome menu to appear. If nothing happens – i.e. if Autoplay is disabled for that drive – double-click the drive icon in My Computer to manually launch the CD-ROM.

2

- *Next*

This launches the Transfer Files and Settings Wizard. As the dialogue box suggests, now is a good time to close any other running programs in order to concentrate on the task at hand.

3

- *Other*
- *Next*

If you were moving files and settings to a different computer, it would help to have them connected with a cable or in a network. Here, however, we simply need to save this computer's configuration in order to reinstate it later. Select the Other option and browse to a suitable location for the resultant file. Your My Documents folder is as good a place as any.

❹

🖱️ *Select an option*

🖱️ *Next*

Do you want to preserve the general appearance of your computer, including the Desktop and program settings, or just specific files and folders, or both? Make your choices here. Be sure to check Let me select a custom list before proceeding.

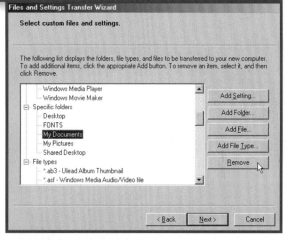

❺

🖱️ *Select options*

🖱️ *Next*

You are now presented with a full and detailed list of everything the wizard can safeguard. Add or remove folders and elements from the suggestions to suit. If in any doubt, leave things in rather than take them out, but do remember the comment about restricting the size of the wizard's file to sensible limits unless you have a network. Including, say, the My Documents folder means that every file and sub-folder located inside it will be copied. Also exclude files or settings relating to programs that you do not intend to use in Windows XP.

❻

🖱️ *Finish*

The Wizard busies itself collecting all the requisite files and settings. These are compiled into a single file (or, to be precise, a single folder with a .UNC extension containing two files) in the location you specified in Step 3 above. Close the wizard when prompted. Now copy this file to a CD-R disc or Zip disk or whatever backup device and media you happen to have, or transfer it across your network to another computer for safe-keeping. We will see it again on p23–24.

PART **1** Over-the-top upgrade

Once you have run the Files and Settings Wizard, backed up all your files and checked that the backup is actually accessible (i.e. not corrupted), it is safe to install Windows XP. In this first method, we will install XP straight over an existing version of Windows.

Pros and cons

On the upside, existing files, folders, programs and system settings are preserved through an over-the-top upgrade. This means that you can hit the ground running without having to reinstall software or spend the next two weeks setting up Windows to your liking. You can also uninstall XP and revert to your previous version. The downside is that any current problems with your computer may be carried through wholesale. Don't assume that an over-the-top installation will necessarily cure your PC of a pre-existing condition like a failure to start or shut down properly or, in particular, a virus infection.

```
                        ┌─────────┐
                        │ Windows │
                        └─────────┘

  A fatal exception 0E has occurred at 0028:C0011E36 in UXD UMM(01) +
  00010E36. The current application will be terminated.

  *  Press any key to terminate the current application.
  *  Press CTRL+ALT+DEL again to restart your computer. You will
     lose any unsaved information in all applications.

                    Press any key to continue
```

If your computer routinely crashes, don't assume that an over-the-top upgrade to XP will fix it. If you are unable to establish and eliminate the underlying problem, a clean XP installation is preferable.

In this example, we will upgrade Windows Me to Windows XP Home Edition. The process is identical starting from Windows 98 or 2000. Before beginning, disable your antivirus program and any other system-level utilities. Refer back to p13–14 and ensure that you have uninstalled any programs or hardware devices that you know (or suspect) to be incompatible with XP. Finally, connect to your Internet Service Provider and open an internet connection.

1

Install Windows XP

Launch Setup from within Windows Me. Pop the XP CD-ROM in the drive and wait for the Welcome screen to appear, or launch it manually as in Step 1 on p18. This time, go straight for the Install button.

Welcome to Microsoft Windows XP

What do you want to do?

→ Install Windows XP
→ Perform additional tasks
→ Check system compatibility

☒ Exit

2

Upgrade (Recommended)

Next

Accept the default Upgrade suggestion in the Installation Type dropdown box and proceed. Just to be crystal clear here about what an upgrade means: we are about to replace the existing, working version of Windows with Window XP. The old Windows will no longer function when we are through (although it can be reinstated if necessary – see p37).

Windows Setup

Welcome to Windows Setup

Which type of installation do you want to perform?

Installation Type: Upgrade (Recommended) ▼

Choose this option to automatically upgrade your current version of Windows.

Upgrading preserves your installed programs, data files, and existing computer settings.

During Setup, it is normal for your screen to go blank for a few seconds and for the computer to restart itself several times.

< Back   Next >   Cancel

3

I accept this agreement

Next

No choice here. Refuse to accept the licence agreement and Setup will simply stop. Read it first if you like.

Windows Setup

License Agreement

Review the terms for using Windows.

Please read the following License Agreement. Use the scroll bar or press the Page Down key to see the rest of the agreement. To continue setting up Windows, you must accept the agreement.

MICROSOFT WINDOWS XP HOME EDITION

END-USER LICENSE AGREEMENT FOR MICROSOFT SOFTWARE

IMPORTANT-READ CAREFULLY: This End-User License Agreement ("EULA") is a legal agreement between you (either an individual or a single entity) and Microsoft Corporation for the Microsoft software that accompanies this

○ I accept this agreement
○ I don't accept this agreement

< Back   Next >   Cancel

4

Product key

Enter the Windows XP Product Key. This is printed on a yellow sticker on the back of the folder that contained the installation CD. If you make a mistake, Setup will stop and prompt you to try again.

Windows Setup

Your Product Key

Type the unique product key for your copy of Windows.

PRODUCT KEY: The 25-character product key appears on a yellow sticker on the back of your Windows CD folder.

Product key:

JJB86 - 75VD6 - ⬚ - ⬚ - ⬚

< Back   Next >   Cancel

5

○ *Show me hardware issues . . .*

⊙ *Next*

Setup now offers to compile a report of hardware and software 'issues' i.e. potential problems and incompatibilities with XP. Accept the recommended suggestion. Bear in mind that you should already have run the Upgrade Advisor (see p14).

6

○ *Yes, download the updated Setup files (Recommended)*

⊙ *Next*

Here, Setup asks permission to download any modified installation files. This is well worth doing as it can save you fussing with updates and patches later, but does require that you have an open internet connection – which is why we suggest that you connect to your ISP before installation. Connect now if you haven't already done so.

7

Setup readies itself to upgrade Windows, and restarts the computer. When you see the Press any key to boot from CD prompt, ignore it. Setup has already copied the files it needs to your hard drive. Shortly after, you are given an opportunity to cancel the current installation. Ignore this too and let Setup restart of its own accord.

8

Eventually, Setup gets down to the real business. There's nothing much to do here so let it continue uninterrupted. Setup inherits your existing Windows settings – time, date, regional settings and so on – as and when required and does not require manual input.

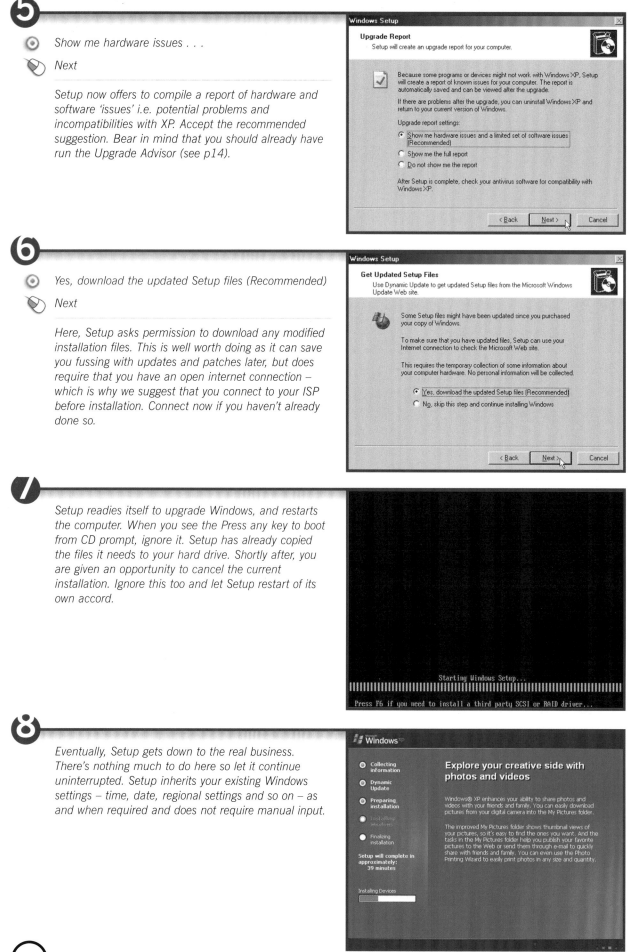

9

⦿ *No, remind me every few days*

🖱 *Next*

We suggest that you don't 'activate' Windows immediately (see p35). Once a particular copy of XP has been activated, it is tied to your computer in its current configuration. If, a week down the line, you decide to install this copy of XP in a new disk partition, on a different hard drive, or even on a different computer, you may find yourself having to telephone Microsoft to explain your actions.

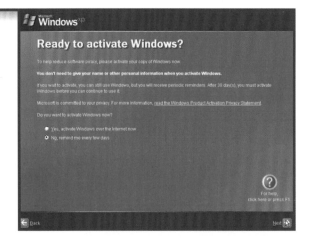

10

⌨ *Your name*

⌨ *Other user names*

🖱 *Next*

User Accounts are an integral part of Windows XP and this is one opportunity to set them up. You can always add more later, or delete existing accounts, but for now type in your own name and that of anybody else who will be using the computer. If you already use the weaker form of User Accounts in Windows Me, you should see existing user names listed here.

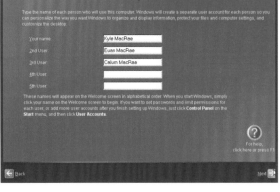

11

🖱 *Finish*

🖱 *Your name*

In the next screen, click Finish to conclude the installation. If you have more than one User Account, Windows XP launches the Welcome screen. Click your name or associated naff icon to log on to Windows. If there is only one account, Windows proceeds directly to the Desktop. This Desktop looks rather different to the one you left behind but you should find that your files, folders, programs and main system settings have survived the upgrade. Do check.

12

🖱 *Start*

🖱 *All Programs*

🖱 *Accessories*

🖱 *System Tools*

🖱 *Files and Settings Transfer Wizard*

The following steps are optional. If you find that your files and settings have indeed been preserved, skip them. If not, or if you want to make certain, retrieve the Files and Settings Transfer Wizard file that you saved earlier and copy it to your new Desktop. Now launch the wizard from the Start menu.

13

- *Next*
- *New computer*
- *Next*
- *I don't need the Wizard Disk*
- *Next*

Tell the wizard that you want to transfer settings to, not from, this computer (it is of course the same computer you started with but the wizard doesn't care). Because you have already copied the folder to your Desktop, you can skip the Wizard Disk step.

Files and Settings Transfer Wizard

Do you have a Windows XP CD?

You will also need to run this wizard on your old computer. You can either create a wizard disk to use on your old computer, or use the wizard from the Windows XP CD.

To create a Wizard Disk, insert a blank, formatted disk into this computer's disk drive. Make sure the old computer has the same type of drive.

- ○ I want to create a Wizard Disk in the following drive:
  - 3½ Floppy (A:)
- ○ I already have a Wizard Disk
- ○ I will use the wizard from the Windows XP CD
- ⦿ I don't need the Wizard Disk. I have already collected my files and settings from my old computer.

< Back   Next >   Cancel

14

- *Other*
- *Browse*
- *Select folder*
- *OK*
- *Next*

Browse to the Files and Settings folder on your Desktop and click OK. The wizard now applies your saved settings and reinstalls saved files. The time this takes depends on the size and complexity of the original .UNC file.

Files and Settings Transfer Wizard

Where are the files and settings?

Where should the wizard look for the items you collected?

- ○ Direct cable (a cable th
- ○ Floppy drive or other re
  - 3½ Floppy (A:)
- ⦿ Other (for example, a re

Browse For Folder

Select a folder

- Desktop
  - ⊞ My Documents
  - ⊞ My Computer
  - ⊞ My Network Places
  - USMT2.UNC

Make New Folder   OK   Cancel

15

- *Finish*
- *OK*

As the wizard finishes, you are prompted to log off Windows. Agree to this. When you log back on, double-check that all is as it should be. If you carried forward User Accounts from Windows Me or 2000 in Step 10, log in as each in turn and run the wizard again, selecting the appropriate .UNC file each time. You must also reset all user passwords, as these are not preserved through an upgrade.

Files and Settings Transfer Wizard

Completing the Files and Settings Transfer Wizard

You have successfully transferred your files and settings from your old computer to your new computer.

To close this wizard, click Finish.

< Back   Finish   Cancel

16

- *Start*
- *My Computer*
- *My Network Places*
- *Set up a home or small office network*
- *Next*

Finally, although a Windows XP upgrade should preserve internet connections and network settings, you may need to run the Network Setup Wizard to reactivate them. This also gives you the chance to configure the basic firewall included in XP. We will look at this wizard in more detail on p84–87.

Network Setup Wizard

Welcome to the Network Setup Wizard

This wizard will help you set up this computer to run on your network. With a network you can:

- Share an Internet connection
- Set up Internet Connection Firewall
- Share files and folders
- Share a printer

To continue, click Next.

< Back   Next >   Cancel

PART ① # Multi-boot installation

If you would prefer to leave your existing Windows setup unchanged and install a 'clean' copy of Windows XP, one attractive option is a multi-boot configuration. Here you can install Windows XP alongside your original version of Windows without any interference or contact between the two; you simply choose which operating system to run every time you restart your computer. The main advantage is the guarantee that you can still use all your old hardware and programs regardless of how Windows XP reacts to them i.e. you can simply run your old version of Windows.

Multi-boot considerations

For this to work, it is necessary either to split your hard disk into two (or more) disk partitions or to install a second physical hard disk.

Windows XP requires a disk partition of at least 1.5GB. However, this would allow you no room for installing programs, saving files and future expansion. Windows also needs a good deal of room for optional features like Hibernation (p153) and System Restore (p155) and, if you use XP's built-in CD burning feature, it requires up to 700MB of disk space every time it creates a new CD (files destined for burning are first duplicated and held in a staging area). Depending upon how much free space you have on your hard disk, create a partition of at least 5GB. With a secondary hard disk drive, the problem will not arise.

Here we will install Windows XP in a fresh hard disk partition that has been created in readiness. The procedure for installing on a separate hard disk is identical; just be very, very sure to specify the correct destination in Step 5.

New Installation (Advanced)

Next

As in Steps 1 and 2 on p21, load the Windows XP CD-ROM from within Windows but this time select New Installation from the Setup menu. Enter the Product Key when prompted in the next screen and continue. The installation procedure from now on is much the same as described already so we will only highlight the points of difference.

2

🖱️ *Advanced Options*

🔘 *I want to choose the install drive letter and partition during Setup*

🖱️ *OK*

This is the critical bit! When you see the Setup Options window, be certain to click the Advanced Options button and tick the drive letter box. If you don't, Setup will overwrite your existing version of Windows as if this was a straightforward over-the-top upgrade.

3

🖱️ *Language*

🖱️ *Next*

Here you should also tell Windows which language you intend to use. US English is the default, naturally, but there is a UK option.

4

⌨️ [Enter]

Setup now runs through its preparatory motions. Eventually, you'll see a grey-on-blue screen inviting you to install Windows XP. Hit the Enter key to proceed.

5

⌨️ *Select partition*

⌨️ [Enter]

This is the point at which you select the disk partition. Here, C: drive contains the old version of Windows, and we wish to install XP in the fresh 10GB partition (D: drive). Select your target drive or disk partition with the keyboard's arrow keys and press Enter.

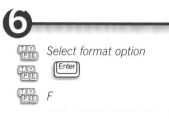

6

⌨ *Select format option*

⌨ [Enter]

⌨ *F*

Setup asks you how to format the partition. Windows XP is better suited to NTFS than FAT32 (see p33) so either opt for a quick NTFS format now or leave it until later if you prefer (see p34). You could go for a full format rather than the quick option but this is only really necessary when installing Windows on a new and untested hard disk rather than a fresh partition on a disk that you know to be okay. Press the F key to confirm your intentions when prompted.

7

🖱 *Customize*

🖱 *Details*

🖱 *Next*

Setup continues. Soon enough, it restarts your computer and switches to the graphical mode we saw in the over-the-top installation. The procedure is largely the same, but your input is required at a couple of later stages. In the Regional and Language Settings screen, set your chosen time zone and keyboard layout

8

⌨ *Name*

⌨ *Company (if applicable)*

🖱 *Next*

Now tell Windows who you are and, if you like, who you work for. This information will later be used to personalise your programs.

9

⌨ *Name*

🖱 *Next*

You can even give your computer a name if you like. The default suggestion is fine unless you intend to set up a network, in which case something snappier might suit.

10

- *Options*
- *Date and time*
- *Next*

  Now set the date, current time and your time zone.

11

- *Typical Settings*
- *Next*

  A little later – installation is a slow business – Setup ask for confirmation of your network settings. The default suggestion is fine for a home network and can be modified later if required. Finally, let Setup continue on its merry way undisturbed.

12

- *Option*
- *Next*

  Here you can take the first step towards setting up a home network and/or an internet connection. However, this can all be left until later if you prefer (see p80-87). In the following screens you will also be prompted to activate Windows now (say no) and enter User Account names (see Step 10 on p23).

13

- *Finish*

  The computer restarts and launches Windows XP. This is the time to run the Files and Settings Transfer Wizard to copy across information from your old version of Windows (see Steps 12–16 on p23–24). Speaking of which…

14

Select version of Windows

[Enter]

When you first restart Windows, and from now on, you will be presented with a multi-boot menu. Here you select which copy of Windows to run: your old version or Windows XP. You can alternate between these every time you reboot the computer.

```
Please select the operating system to start:

    Microsoft Windows XP Home Edition
    Microsoft Windows

Use the up and down arrow keys to move the highlight to your choice.
Press ENTER to choose.
Seconds until highlighted choice will be started automatically: 23




For troubleshooting and advanced startup options for Windows, press F8.
```

15

Start

Control Panel

Performance and Maintenance

System

Advanced Settings

Default operating system

OK

One operating system is always designated the default, which means it loads automatically after a short delay if the computer is left unattended. If you like, you can reset both the default and the delay here.

Startup and Recovery

System startup

Default operating system:

"Microsoft Windows XP Home Edition" /fastdetect

"Microsoft Windows XP Home Edition" /fastdetect
"Microsoft Windows"

☑ Time to display recovery options when needed: 30 ⏵ seconds

To edit the startup options file manually, click Edit.   [Edit]

System failure

☑ Write an event to the system log

☑ Send an administrative alert

☑ Automatically restart

Write debugging information

Small memory dump (64 KB)

Small dump directory:

%SystemRoot%\Minidump

☑ Overwrite any existing file

[OK]   [Cancel]

? QUICK Q & A

I only have one hard disk. How do I create a separate partition for Windows XP so that I can run two operating systems side-by-side?

Invest in a specialist partitioning utility like PartitionMagic from PowerQuest (www.powerquest.com). Although FDISK can split a hard disk into two or more partitions, it destroys all existing data in the process i.e. your current copy of Windows will be lost. This rather defeats the purpose.

PowerQuest PartitionMagic 7.0

General   View   Operations   Tools   Wizards   Help

Disks

☐ My Computer
  ☐ Disk 1 - 16378 MB
    ■ C:CONNECTIX
  ☐ *:Extended
    ■ D:

Disk 1 - 16378 MB

C: CONNECTIX
6,377.3 MB FAT32

D:
10,001.4 MB   FAT32

Disk	Partition	Type	Size MB	Used MB	Unused MB	Status	Pri/Log
1	C:CONNECTIX	■ FAT32	6,377.3	647.4	5,729.9	Active	Primary
1	*:	☐ Extended	10,001.4	10,001.4	0.0	None	Primary
1	D:	■ FAT32	10,001.4	9.8	9,991.6	None	Logical

Create new partition   Resize partitions   Redistribute free space   Merge partitions   Copy partition   Exit

☐ FAT ■ FAT32 ■ NTFS ■ Linux Ext2 ■ Linux Swap ■ NetWare ■ HPFS ☐ Extended ■ Unallocated ■ Unformatted ☐ Used ☐ Unused

We recommend closing all other applications while running PartitionMagic.   0 operations pending

WINDOWS XP

Clean installation

In some circumstances, the best or indeed the only option is a fresh installation of Windows XP. This is a very similar process to the multi-boot configuration described earlier, with the difference that you have no choice over which operating system to boot.

In the following scenario, we will assume that you have installed a new hard disk drive in your computer. Alternatively, you could achieve precisely the same starting point by formatting the existing drive i.e. completely wiping it of all data, including Windows. This is best achieved with a DOS utility called FDISK, which is included on a standard Windows boot floppy disk. Alternatively, you can use the partitioning tools included on the Windows XP CD-ROM. For full details, see Microsoft Knowledge Base articles 255867 and 313348 (go to http://support.microsoft.com and enter 255867 or 313348 in the search field).

Do not forget to back up everything you wish to keep and run the Files and Settings Transfer Wizard before formatting the disk. We also suggest making a note of your internet connection and network settings.

Whereas in the two installation options above we began working from within Windows, here we can run Setup directly from the bootable Windows CD-ROM.

1

The first, critical task is to configure your computer to boot from the CD drive (or DVD drive – it comes to the same thing) rather than the hard disk. This means dipping into BIOS to make and save the changes (see Quick Q & A on p32). You will later reverse this and reinstate the hard disk as the default boot device.

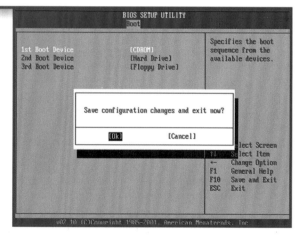

2

Put the Windows XP installation CD-ROM in the drive and restart your computer. Setup will launch. Once it has examined your system, it should invite you to proceed.

❸

TYPE [F8]

Now press the F8 key to confirm that you have read and agree to the license agreement. Use the Page Down key if you really want to read it.

```
Windows XP Licensing Agreement

Microsoft Windows XP Home Edition

END-USER LICENSE AGREEMENT

IMPORTANT-READ CAREFULLY: This End-User
License Agreement ("EULA") is a legal agreement between you
(either an individual or a single entity) and Microsoft
Corporation for the Microsoft software product identified above,
which includes computer software and may include associated
media, printed materials, "online" or electronic documentation,
and Internet-based services ("Product").    An amendment or
addendum to this EULA may accompany the Product.  YOU AGREE TO BE
BOUND BY THE TERMS OF THIS EULA BY
INSTALLING, COPYING, OR OTHERWISE USING THE
PRODUCT. IF YOU DO NOT AGREE, DO NOT INSTALL
OR USE THE PRODUCT; YOU MAY RETURN IT TO YOUR
PLACE OF PURCHASE FOR A FULL REFUND.

  1. GRANT OF LICENSE. Microsoft grants you the following rights
     provided that you comply with all terms and conditions of
     this EULA:

     * Installation and use.  You may install, use, access,
       display and run one copy of the Product on a single
       computer, such as a workstation, terminal or other device
       ("Workstation Computer").   [a] The Product may not
       be used by more than one (1) processor at any one time

F8=I agree   ESC=I do not agree   PAGE DOWN=Next Page
```

❹

TYPE [Enter]

Because this is an Upgrade rather than a Full Windows XP CD-ROM (see p13), Setup refuses to continue until it sees evidence of an earlier version of Windows. Remove the XP disc for now, pop a qualifying CD-ROM in the drive and press Enter.

```
Windows XP Home Edition Setup

Setup cannot find a previous version of Windows installed on
your computer. To continue, Setup needs to verify that you
qualify to use this upgrade product.

Please insert your Windows NT 3.51 Workstation, Windows NT 4.0
Workstation, Windows 2000 Professional, Windows 95, Windows 98, or
Windows Millennium CD into your CD-ROM drive.

  * When the CD is in the drive, press ENTER.

  * To quit Setup, press F3.

ENTER=Continue   F3=Quit
```

❺

TYPE *Select Option*
TYPE [Enter]

Next, tell Setup where to install XP. If you only have one hard drive and it hasn't been partitioned, there is no room for confusion here. Otherwise, see Step 5 on p26 and select the appropriate target.

```
Windows XP Home Edition Setup

The following list shows the existing partitions and
unpartitioned space on this computer.

Use the UP and DOWN ARROW keys to select an item in the list.

  * To set up Windows XP on the selected item, press ENTER.

  * To create a partition in the unpartitioned space, press C.

  * To delete the selected partition, press D.

16379 MB Disk 0 at Id 0 on bus 0 on atapi [MBR]
     Unpartitioned space                16379 MB

ENTER=Install   C=Create Partition   F3=Quit
```

❻

TYPE *Select Option*
TYPE [Enter]

The hard disk (or disk partition) must now be formatted. Choose NTFS. The 'Quick' option bypasses disk scanning and could result in problems if the disk has bad sectors (duff spots). A full format takes longer but identifies and avoids any bad sectors. Unless you're confident that your disk is physically sound – e.g. it has previously run Windows – go for a full format.

```
Windows XP Home Edition Setup

A new partition for Windows XP has been created on

16379 MB Disk 0 at Id 0 on bus 0 on atapi [MBR].

This partition must now be formatted.

From the list below, select a file system for the new partition.
Use the UP and DOWN ARROW keys to select the file system you want,
and then press ENTER.

If you want to select a different partition for Windows XP,
press ESC.

  Format the partition using the NTFS file system (Quick)
  Format the partition using the FAT file system (Quick)
  Format the partition using the NTFS file system
  Format the partition using the FAT file system

ENTER=Continue   ESC=Cancel
```

7

You will be prompted to replace the Windows XP CD in the drive at this point. Setup then formats the disk according to your selection in Step 6.

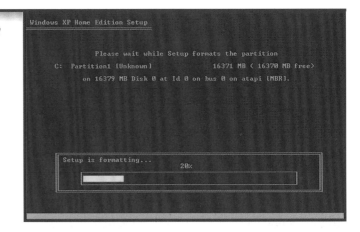

8

Setup now copies files to the hard disk and proceeds in an identical manner to the multi-boot scenario already described. When XP launches, remember to run the Files and Settings Transfer Wizard. Also return to BIOS and make the hard disk the default boot device.

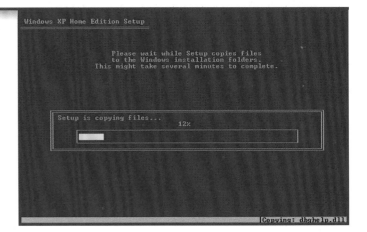

?

QUICK Q & A

How do I get into the BIOS?
BIOS, Basic Input/Output System, is a set of instructions and drivers embedded in a chip on the motherboard that gets a computer up and running before Windows takes over. To access the BIOS Setup program, you must press a specific key as the computer is powering up. Your motherboard manual should make this clear but it is usually Delete, Escape, F1 or F2. You may also see a helpful Press DEL to enter SETUP or similar message on screen.

Once in BIOS Setup, look for an option called Advanced BIOS features, or similar. Here you will find drives listed in the order in which they are examined by BIOS during startup. To boot from the CD or DVD drive, you must temporarily make it the first drive in the chain. BIOS menus are accessed and controlled with the keyboard, not the mouse, but you should find on-screen instructions. When you have reordered the drives, save your changes before rebooting. The computer will now examine the CD/DVD drive for a bootable program – in this case, Windows Setup on the Windows XP installation CD-ROM – before doing anything else.

PART **1** FAT or NTFS?

A file system is a kind of organisational office manager for data on a computer. Whenever you create and save a file, the file system remembers its physical location on the hard disk; when you later wish to retrieve that file, the file system knows just where to look. It's all vastly more complicated than that, of course, right down to the microscopic magnetic level, but what matters for the successful operation of your computer is that your hard disk is managed by the best possible file system. This in turn depends upon the operating system.

A file system keeps tabs on binary data as it shifts from one sector on the hard disk to another. It is quite remarkable that it keeps track of every last 1 and 0 over the days, months and years, but we demand no less from it..

As we have seen, Windows XP invites you to change the file system from FAT (File Allocation Table) to NTFS (New Technology File System) during an upgrade – unless, of course, you are upgrading from Windows NT or 2000 and already use NTFS. However, thanks to backwards compatibility, Windows XP also runs quite happily under FAT32. This means you have a choice – so is it worth switching to NTFS?

In fact, there are several benefits with NTFS:
● Support for larger hard disks
● Support for larger files
● Increased security and reliability (including file encryption and file-level access permissions in Windows XP Professional).

However, there are also a couple of caveats:
● You cannot change an NTFS disk to FAT32 without reformatting it first. This means scrubbing all your files and wiping Windows.
● An operating system running on a FAT32 hard disk or disk partition is unable to 'see' NTFS disks or partitions. This means that if, for instance, you install Windows XP on an NTFS partition alongside Windows Me in a FAT32 partition, you could not access any files stored on the XP partition from within Me.
● Converting to NTFS rules out uninstalling XP and reverting to your previous FAT-based operating system (see p37).

These considerations aside, NTFS is the unequivocal file system of choice for Windows XP. If you opted out of NTFS during installation or upgraded directly from a version of Windows running Windows XP under FAT32 and you would like to upgrade now, here's what to do.

Historically, here are the recommended file systems for each main Windows release:

File system	Windows version
FAT16	Windows 95
FAT32	Windows 95 OSR2, Windows 98 & 98SE, Windows Me
NTFS	Windows NT, Windows 2000, Windows XP

1

🖱️ *My Computer*

🖱️ *Local Disk C:*

🖱️ *Properties*

First, establish for sure which file system you are currently using. Select the disk or disk partition in My Computer and look in the General tab of the Properties screen. In this case, it is FAT32.

Local Disk (C:) Properties

General | Tools | Hardware | Sharing

Type: Local Disk
File system: FAT32

■ Used space: 2,469,494,784 bytes   2.29 GB
■ Free space: 14,700,642,304 bytes   13.6 GB

Capacity: 17,170,137,088 bytes   15.9 GB

Drive C   [Disk Cleanup]

[OK] [Cancel] [Apply]

2

🖱️ *Start*

🖱️ *Run*

⌨️ *convert c: /fs:ntfs*

🖱️ *OK*

This launches the Windows Convert.exe utility. It's not often that you have to use the command prompt like this in Windows XP but this is the only way to do it.

Run

Type the name of a program, folder, document, or Internet resource, and Windows will open it for you.

Open: | convert c: /fs:ntfs |

[OK] [Cancel] [Browse...]

3

⌨️ Y

⌨️ [Enter]

⌨️ Y

⌨️ [Enter]

⌨️ Y

⌨️ [Enter]

Answer yes to any prompts. Because the utility cannot modify a file system while it is in use (i.e. by Windows), the conversion will be scheduled to commence next time you restart the computer.

4

Upon restart, Windows checks the integrity of the hard disk and proceeds with the conversion. This simple process upgrades the file system to NTFS without any loss of data.

PART 1 Product Activation

You probably know all about this already but just to reiterate: Windows XP will only work for 30 days unless you 'activate' it with Microsoft over the internet or by telephone. Windows itself is not shy of reminding of you about this so, unless your PC came pre-activated by the manufacturer, you will be bombarded with balloons popping up from the Notification Area. Click a balloon at any time to activate Windows.

Leave it too late and eventually you will find that Windows halts at the Welcome screen in a most unwelcome manner and forces you to activate before you can proceed.

There is no need to tell Microsoft who you are or how you acquired your copy of Windows XP, but Product Activation 'locks' your copy of Windows to your computer. You cannot sell or lend your Windows XP CD to a friend, and nor can you install the same copy on more than one computer at the same time. This is precisely the kind of 'casual' piracy that Product Activation is intended to tackle.

Should you wish to install Windows XP afresh on a new system, the licence dictates that you must first uninstall it from the original machine. When you then install it on the new system, Product Activation will (probably) fail, at which point you have to telephone Microsoft to explain your actions. It's all rather frustrating, especially when there is no automatic deactivation procedure to wipe the slate clean and free up a copy of Windows XP for a fresh installation. Still, having contacted Microsoft operators many times – quite legitimately – we have yet to be refused a new code with which to reactivate a copy of Windows XP.

You can of course reinstall Windows XP on the same computer as often as you like, and reactivation should not be required. However, if you make multiple, significant and near-simultaneous hardware changes – install a new hard disk, video card, network card, CD drive, additional memory and swap the processor – this can throw a spanner in the works. Windows XP may suspect that it is no longer installed on the same computer, stop working and demand re-activation.

Much can be said for and against Product Activation in principle but in practice it is quick, painless and private.

Lest you forget, Windows constantly reminds you to activate Windows.

A bit of a no-brainer: either activate Windows XP now or stop using it.

If you try to activate a copy of Windows XP a second time on a different computer, you will have to convince Microsoft that you are not in breach of the licence agreement.

QUICK Q & A

How do I turn off those annoying popup balloons?
The easiest way is with TweakUI (see p151). Look in the Taskbar section and uncheck Enable balloon tips. The Notification Area will now leave you in peace.

1

Yes, let's activate Windows over the internet now

Next

Launch the Product Activation wizard by clicking one of the reminder balloons or from the Start menu (Activate Windows appears as the top entry in the first column of the All Programs menu). If you don't have an internet connection, select the telephone option instead.

2

No

Next

You can register as a Microsoft customer if you want to but there's no necessity to do so and bypassing registration speeds things up.

3

OK

That's it. This copy of Windows XP is now inextricably linked to your current hardware.

4

Confirmation ID

If you opt to telephone Microsoft rather than take the automated internet route, this is what you will see. Call the free number and, when prompted, enter the 54-digit Installation ID code on your telephone keypad (assuming you have a touch-tone phone). You then need to enter the proffered Confirmation ID code in boxes A through to G. The whole thing takes around five minutes.

WINDOWS XP Uninstalling XP

If you perform an over-the-top upgrade on Windows 98 or Me – but not on NT or 2000, unfortunately – it is possible to uninstall Windows XP completely and revert to your original operating system.

Before doing so, be sure to back up any files you have created in the meantime. You will also have to reinstall any programs that you installed under XP post-upgrade, although any programs that were carried forward from your earlier operating system to XP should be preserved.

Note that you can only do this if you have not changed the file system from FAT32 to NTFS in the meantime (see p34).

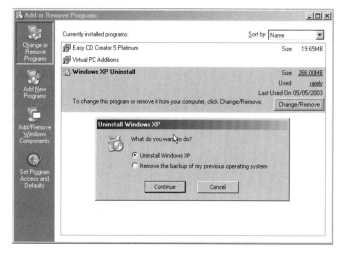

In Safe Mode, you can uninstall Windows XP in its entirety.

First, log on to Windows in Safe Mode as 'the' Administrator (see p94).

- *Start*
- *Control Panel*
- *Add or Remove Programs*
- *Windows XP Uninstall*

Follow the wizard. When the computer reboots, you will be back where you started pre-upgrade.

Override the warning to complete an uninstall of Windows XP.

Without further ado, Windows XP self-destructs and returns you to your original system.

PART **2** WINDOWS XP
Three fresh faces

WINDOWS XP

The Desktop

The default Windows XP Desktop is nothing if not spartan. In a clean installation, the only visible elements are the Recycle Bin icon, the Taskbar, the Start button, a clock and an inactive Windows Messenger icon. Let us take a tour.

The Recycle Bin: temporary storage area for deleted files and the only default icon on the XP Desktop

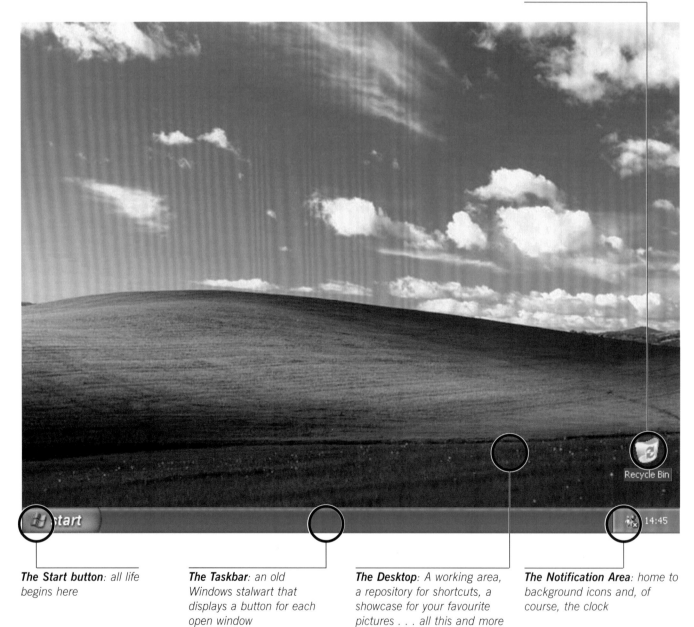

The Start button: *all life begins here*

The Taskbar: *an old Windows stalwart that displays a button for each open window*

The Desktop: *A working area, a repository for shortcuts, a showcase for your favourite pictures . . . all this and more*

The Notification Area: *home to background icons and, of course, the clock*

Desktop Cleanup Wizard

Newly-installed programs are wont to plant shortcut icons all over the Desktop, and you may contribute to the clutter with your own files and folders. Of course, the Desktop is really just a folder itself (albeit one that cannot be deleted) and makes an ideal repository for shortcuts and short-term storage. But tempting though it is to save just about every new file or download directly to the Desktop, it is better practice to use the My Documents folder for long-term file storage and reserve the Desktop for use as a temporary working space.

Windows XP attempts to maintain order with the Desktop Cleanup Wizard. You will first encounter this as a popup balloon emanating from the Notification Area on the Taskbar (located at the far right end, home to the clock).

If you click the bubble, Windows scans the Desktop for seldom-used shortcuts and relegates them to a new Desktop folder called Unused Desktop Shortcuts.

You can access them from here at any time. The wizard also lets you deselect shortcuts that you would rather keep within sight.

Windows XP periodically reminds you to perform certain tasks by means of really helpful/intensely irritating (delete as appropriate) popup messages.

If an icon has an arrow-in-a-box, you know it is a shortcut and not an actual 'thing'.

Make sure that Windows doesn't hide shortcuts that you would rather have handy on the Desktop.

To launch the Desktop Cleanup Wizard manually rather than waiting for it to appear every couple of months,

 anywhere on the Desktop

Arrange Icons By

Run Desktop Cleanup Wizard

The manual route to the Desktop Cleanup Wizard.

Hide Desktop icons

For the trimmest possible Desktop,

A Desktop toolbar keeps hidden
icons within reach.

- 🖱️ *any blank spot on the desktop*
- 🖱️ *Arrange Icons By*
- ⭕ *Show Desktop Icons*

*This leaves the Desktop completely clear, which is ideal
if you like to display a full-screen background image
unencumbered with icons.*

In order to access your Desktop icons when they are hidden from
sight, the easiest way is to include a Desktop toolbar on the
Taskbar. We're skipping ahead slightly here (see p52) but

- 🖱️ *a clear spot on the Taskbar*
- 🖱️ *Toolbars*
- 🖱️ *Desktop*

*This puts a link to the Desktop on the Taskbar. Click the
chevrons for a popup list containing all hidden Desktop
icons (including the Unused folder).*

Change icons

Desktop icons can be customised in several ways. The first and
most obvious step might be to change them altogether.

- 🖱️ *any icon*
- 🖱️ *Properties*
- 🖱️ *Shortcut tab*
- 🖱️ *Change Icon*

Select an alternative from the choices on offer

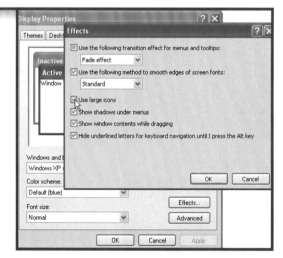

*You can create and use your own
icons if you prefer; simply save
any image as 32 x 32 pixels and
give it a .BMP extension.*

Make icons bigger

If you use a high screen resolution and get a headache trying to
work out which tiny icon is which, try this:

- 🖱️ *the Desktop*
- 🖱️ *Properties*
- 🖱️ *Appearance tab*
- 🖱️ *Effects*
- ⦿ *Use Large Icons*

*Super-size your icons and give
your eyes a break.*

Rearrange Desktop icons

🖱 the Desktop

🖱 Arrange Icons By

🖱 Choose options for ordering your icons

If you turn off Auto Arrange, you can drag icons to any location on the Desktop instead of having them automatically line up in rows and columns. If you leave Align to Grid selected, they still line up neatly but not necessarily from the left.

Keep slippery icons in formation by pinning them to an invisible grid.

Add icons to the Desktop

Windows XP hides virtually all Desktop icons by default but you may wish to restore a few essentials.

🖱 the Desktop

🖱 Properties

🖱 Desktop tab

🖱 Customise Desktop

⦿ *Check the box next to any or all of My Computer, My Documents, My Network Places and Internet Explorer to restore icons to the Desktop*

Disabuse the Desktop of minimalism.

Create program shortcuts

To place a shortcut to a program on the Desktop,

- 🖱 *Start*
- 🖱 *All Programs*
- 🖱 *any program on the menu*
- 🖱 *Send To*
- 🖱 *Desktop (create shortcut)*

Bypass the Start menu with Desktop shortcuts.

Create file and folder shortcuts

- 🖱 *drag a file or folder from any Explorer window straight to the Desktop and select Create Shortcuts Here from the popup menu as you drop it*

Alternatively,

- 🖱 *the file or folder*
- 🖱 *Send To*
- 🖱 *Desktop (create shortcut)*

A right-button drag-and-drop provides a shortcut to any file, folder or item.

Delete Desktop icons

As ever, you can delete any Desktop icon (or file or folder) by dragging it to the Recycle Bin, where it remains until the Bin is full or you permanently empty it. Remember that deleting a shortcut does not affect the item it points to.

Deleting a program shortcut does not uninstall the program.

The Start menu

Now we really see some changes. The Start menu in Windows Me and other earlier versions of Windows was a skinny, stark affair but here we have a chunky, dual-column menu.

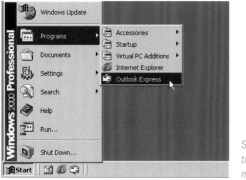

Say goodbye to the stark Start menu of old.

Canny eyes will note that both columns are sub-divided into sections, but it's not immediately obvious why. After a few days of using XP, you might also notice that items on the Start menu begin to shift around but the reasons for this may not be evident either. So what exactly is going on?

Current user

Pinned programs

Most Frequently Used Programs

All Programs

Folder shortcuts

Control Panel link

Help and Support Center

Search utility

Run command

Log off/Turn off buttons

Dissecting the Start menu

The basic anatomy of the Start menu is as follows:

● **Current User** This tells you at a glance who is currently logged on to Windows – a useful reminder when you return to a shared computer and are not sure if another user has logged on in your absence.

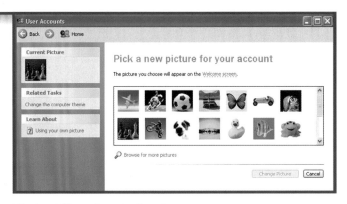

Windows XP's motley selection of user icons is less than inspiring but you can change it in User Accounts (see p91–97) or use one of your own images instead.

● **All Programs** Point at or click this button to see a list of all installed software, and click any program to launch it. Newly-installed programs are highlighted in the menu for a while to aid navigation – a surprisingly useful innovation when the menu eventually spans three or four columns and you can no longer find anything.

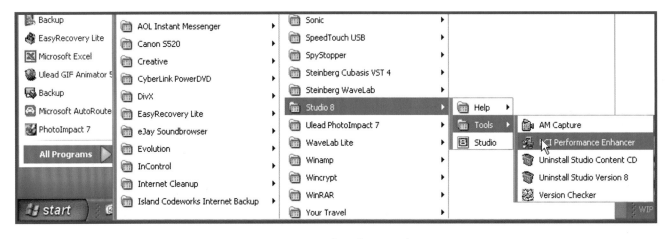

An active computer soon grows a bustling All Programs menu.

● **Most Frequently Used Programs** The programs you use most often appear here to save you scrolling through the full All Programs menu. The list dynamically updates in line with your habits i.e. start using a different program regularly and the least accessed program on the list gets bumped off to make room.

● **Pinned Programs** The programs in this part of the Start menu remain fixed regardless of how frequently you use them. You can, of course, customise this list, as we shall see.

● **Folder shortcuts** The top of the right-hand column provides links to several useful folders, including My Documents.

● **Control Panel** The old Settings menu entry has gone and in its place we find a direct link to the Control Panel.

Add programs to Pinned Programs

With Pinned Programs, you can keep a selection of software within easy reach at all times.

Start

All Programs

any program

Pin to Start menu

Take control of Start menu shortcuts with Pinned Programs.

Add items to the Start menu

Odd though it may seem, you can add any file, folder, shortcut or program to the Start menu. This saves you having to navigate through files and folders or use Desktop shortcuts. Locate your target and then drag it (with the left or right mouse button) straight to the Start button on the Taskbar. Wait just a moment and the Start menu will open. Now drop the item either within the Pinned Programs section or, if you hover above the All Programs button to make it expand, anywhere else. A horizontal black line indicates where the item will land.

Moreover, if you add a folder that contains sub-folders and files to All Programs, its entire contents expand in a series of cascading menus when you point at it. In this way, you can zoom in on any target file without having to work your way through a nested hierarchy of folders in My Documents.

Drag any item to the Start menu for an instant shortcut.

Who needs Explorer when you can do this straight from the Start menu?

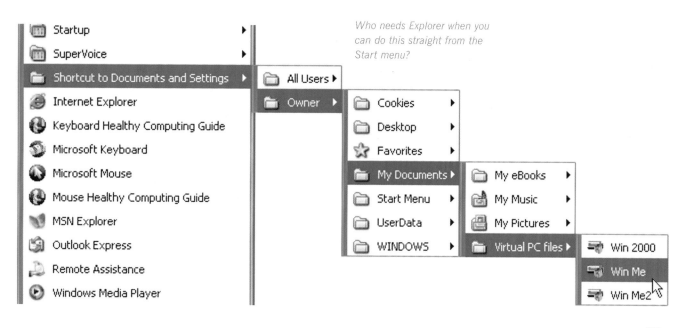

Prune the Start menu

To remove any item from the Pinned Programs list,

 the item

 Remove from This List

You can do exactly the same in the Most Frequently Used Programs section (although you cannot add programs here). To remove an item from the All Programs list,

the item

Delete

This only deletes the shortcut to the program, not the program itself, of course. It is particularly useful when you uninstall a program and it leaves behind a dead link on the menu.

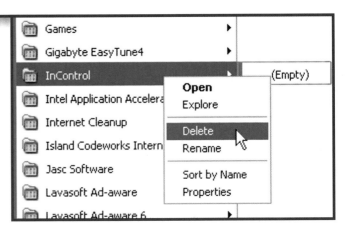

Tidy up after sloppy programs.

Bolster the Most Frequently Used Programs list

The default number of program icons shown in the Most Frequently Used Programs area is six but you can up the number to suit.

the Start button

Properties

Start Menu tab

Customise

General tab

Change the number of programs on the Start Menu

If you opt for 10 or more, be sure to check the Small icons options or else they will not all fit on the Start menu (which rather defeats the purpose). You can also clear the exisiting Most Frequently Used Programs list for a fresh start.

Make the Most Frequently Used Programs menu as long as you like.

Reorder the All Programs list

You can drag and drop any item on the All Programs menu up or down a column or from one column to another. Again, look for the horizontal black line that shows you where it will land. To copy an item to a new location while leaving the original in place, hold down the Control key as you drag. You can also sort the All Programs menu alphabetically by right-clicking any item and selecting Sort by Name from the popup menu.

Make sense of the Start menu with automatic sorting.

Rename menu items

Occasionally, a menu item is lumbered with a less-than-helpful title. You can rename it to something more useful by right-clicking any item in All Programs, Pinned Programs or Most Frequently Used Programs and selecting Rename from the popup menu.

Call a spade a spade, or an aim.exe an Instant Messenger.

Add or remove My Recent Documents

If you choose, the Start menu can host a link to the your most recently accessed documents. This is a useful shortcut – click on any entry and the relevant program fires up and opens your document – but some people are less keen on the privacy implications: anyone who uses your computer can check up on what you have just been doing.

 *Start button*

Properties

Start Menu tab

Start menu

Customize

Advanced tab

List my most recently opened documents

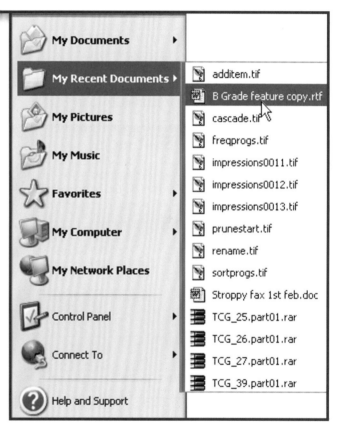

An optional shortcut to work in progress.

Change Control Panel settings

One particular irritant with Windows XP is the revamped Control Panel. We suspect that most experienced Windows users switch from the default Category view back to the familiar – and much more useful – Classic view. However, you can also use the Start menu to access any Control Panel item directly. With this method, merely pointing at Control Panel in the Start menu is sufficient to makes its constituent parts appear in a menu.

You can repeat this feat with My Computer and My Documents to make it easier to locate files and folders without relying upon Desktop shortcuts or Windows Explorer.

Instant access to the Control Panel.

- *Start button*
- *Properties*
- *Start Menu tab*
- *Start menu*
- *Customize*
- *Advanced tab*
- *Display as a menu (this option is located under Control Panel in the Start menu items area)*

Add Favorites to the Start menu

Another useful tip. Instead of firing up your web browser and searching through your bookmarks for a web page, you can place a shortcut to your Favorites folder right on the Start menu and open the page from there. The Favorites folder can also contain links to standard (i.e. non-web) folders and files.

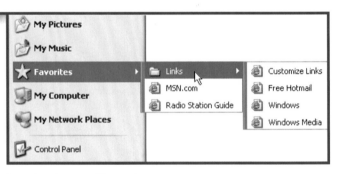

Launch web pages, files and folders with the Favorites menu.

- *Start button*
- *Properties*
- *Start Menu tab*
- *Start menu*
- *Customize*
- *Advanced tab*
- *Favorites menu (this option is in the Start menu items area)*

And finally...

If it all gets too much and you just can't get used to the new-fangled Start menu, revert to the 'Classic' style and pretend that you don't really have Windows XP at all.

- *Start button*
- *Properties*
- ▶ *Start menu tab*
- ▶ *Classic Start menu*

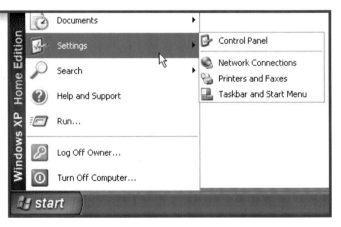

Keeping up (old) appearances with XP in chameleon mode.

PART **2**

The Taskbar (and toolbars)

The Desktop and the Start menu both provide a multitude of shortcuts to files, folders and programs. Most people tend to use one or the other as a starting point, although you can of course customise both and alternate between them. The third main option is the Taskbar and again this familiar Windows feature has been substantially overhauled for Windows XP. Here is a run-through of the features that we have found most useful.

Add toolbars

The Taskbar starts off looking rather sparse but you can deck it out with a range of additional toolbars, each of which offers shortcuts. Right-click any blank spot on the Taskbar, select Toolbars, and check any that you fancy.

Tart up the Taskbar with toolbars.

- **Address** Simply a field in which you can enter a web address to launch it in your default browser. It is also possible to specify the path to a file, folder or program – e.g. My Documents\My Pictures\landscape.jpg – but why bother when clickable shortcut icons are available?

Address http://www.amazon.co.uk/   Go

A web browser-in-miniature on the Taskbar.

- **Links** Essentially a copy of the Links toolbar used in Internet Explorer. Drag any bookmark from your Favorites folder to the Links toolbar to create a handy shortcut. You can also drag standard files and folders to the Links toolbar for added flexibility. Use the right mouse button to drag an icon and select Create Shortcut Here when dropping it in place.

Shortcuts galore with the Links toolbar.

- **Language toolbar** Primarily used for speech recognition, if this feature is installed on your computer, and for swapping between country-specific keyboard layouts.

This toolbar ties in with the Regional and Language Options features in the Control Panel.

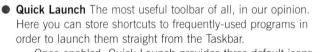

- **Desktop** As mentioned on p42, this generates a popup menu listing all Desktop icons, including the Unused Desktop Shortcuts folder.

This toolbar saves you having to minimise open windows to access Desktop shortcuts.

- **Quick Launch** The most useful toolbar of all, in our opinion. Here you can store shortcuts to frequently-used programs in order to launch them straight from the Taskbar.

    Once enabled, Quick Launch provides three default icons: Internet Explorer, Windows Media Player and Show Desktop. The last one is particularly handy because it instantly minimises all open windows to the Taskbar and reveals the entire Desktop. However, you can also add your own program shortcuts by dragging and dropping any executable file (or shortcut that points to it) directly to the Quick Launch toolbar. Use the right mouse button to copy rather than move the file or shortcut.

    To remove a Quick Launch shortcut, right-click it and select Delete; and to rearrange the order of icons on the toolbar, drag them from one position to another.

▲ *Quick Launch is a customisable toolbar for firing up programs without going through either the Desktop or the Start menu.*

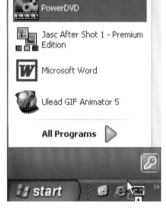

▶ *Here we are dragging a PowerDVD program icon from the Start menu to the Quick Launch toolbar in order to create a shortcut.*

Resize and lock Taskbar toolbars

Busy Taskbar toolbars with lots of icons shrink to save space, thereby hiding some or all of their shortcuts. However, they can be resized: latch on to the toolbar handle – a column of dots at one end – and drag it to the left or right to hide or reveal icons. When a toolbar is in its reduced state, click on the little double chevron to see its full complement in a popup menu.

Windows automatically minimises the Quick Launch toolbar to display only three icons, whereas you may want to keep more within permanent view. First, drag the Quick Launch toolbar to the right to reveal as many icons as you wish, and reorder them if necessary by dragging and dropping. Now right-click any blank spot on the Taskbar and select Lock the Taskbar. The Quick Launch toolbar handles disappear and it will no longer minimise. In fact, locking the Taskbar like this affects all toolbars simultaneously so, if you also use the Desktop and Links toolbars, play around until you find an optimal configuration before freezing them.

▲ *A crowded toolbar can be fully expanded, providing there is room on the Taskbar.*

▶ *Chevrons let you view a toolbar's contents in a popup menu.*

▼ *Freeze the Taskbar to stop toolbars growing and shrinking dynamically.*

Reposition toolbars

With the exception of Quick Launch, you can reposition Taskbar toolbars anywhere on the screen. Minimise all open windows first and unlock the Taskbar if it is currently locked. Now click on any toolbar title. The mouse cursor should change to a double-headed arrow. Drag the toolbar off the Taskbar and on to the Desktop. There it will float in a window. If you move it to the very top or edge of the screen, it will dock there.

Optionally, right-click a floating or docked toolbar and check Always on Top to prevent other windows from covering it. If the toolbar is docked, you can also check Auto Hide to keep it hidden between activities.

Rather than allocate each additional toolbar its own slice of screen space, you can drag one onto another. Thus, for instance, you might dock the Address toolbar and drop Desktop and Links toolbars directly onto it.

The end result is almost akin to having two Taskbars: the standard one at the bottom of the screen with Quick Launch program icons, plus a secondary tool at the top of the screen with which to enter web addresses, access Desktop items and open files and folders.

When the mouse cursor changes like this, you can drag a toolbar away from the Taskbar.

One Taskbar not sufficient? Use movable toolbars to increase your options.

Make your own toolbars

When working on a project that involves lots of related files and sub-folders all stored within a central folder – designing a website, for instance, or writing a computer manual – it makes sense to turn the top-level folder into a custom-made toolbar. This affords you quick access to all your files at any time. Like any other Taskbar toolbar, you can expand, lock, move and dock a custom-built toolbar.

  the Taskbar

Toolbars

New Toolbar

Now browse to your target folder

Any folder can be turned into a toolbar.

Group/ungroup Taskbar buttons

One of the ways in which Windows XP tries to maintain Taskbar
tidiness is by grouping open windows within as few Taskbar
buttons as possible. Thus if you have multiple Word documents
open simultaneously, or two or more instances of the same
application running, or several Explorer windows open (My
Documents, My Computer etc.), or umpteen web pages, only one
button appears on the Taskbar for each group. This button then
expands into a popup menu with each open window numbered.

Button grouping saves Taskbar space.

Like it or loathe it this feature can be turned on or off to suit.
Again,

🖱 *any clear spot on the Taskbar*

🖱 *Properties*

🖱 *Taskbar tab*

⦿◯ *check or uncheck Group similar taskbar buttons*

? QUICK Q & A

**How can I close a whole bunch
of windows at the same time?**
Hold down the Control key and
click each Taskbar button in
turn. When they are all selected,
right-click any one of them and
select Close Group from the
popup menu.

Cascade
Tile Horizontally
Tile Vertically
Minimize Group

Close Group

Resize the Taskbar

Taskbar buttons slide and shrink to make more room available as
the Taskbar fills up but during multitasking it can eventually run
out of space, particularly if you turn off the button-grouping feature.
At this point, the Taskbar displays a pair of up and down arrows.
Click these to toggle between two or more rows of buttons.

This is actually a bit of a pain because it involves an extra click
to access hidden Taskbar buttons. However, you can resize the
Taskbar to accommodate as many buttons as necessary: point at
the upper edge with the mouse cursor, wait for it to change to a
double-headed arrow, and drag upwards. To permanently retain a
double- or triple-height Taskbar, lock it as described on p52.

*When the Taskbar outgrows
itself, its splits into two or more
rows.*

*A double-height Taskbar means
more buttons remain accessible.*

Notification Area

What you might know as the System Tray – the far right end of the Taskbar, home to the clock and the Windows Messenger icon – is now called the Notification Area. Its purpose is to indicate which programs or processes are currently running in the background: an antivirus scanner, an internet connection, a scheduled task etc. To stop the Notification Area encroaching unnecessarily into the Taskbar, Windows shrinks it to hide icons that (it assumes) do not require your active attention.

By and large, this works well, but it can leave you wondering whether, for instance, your antivirus program is really doing the business or has quietly slipped off duty. You can expand the Notification Area to reveal all of its icons by clicking the arrow on its left edge – but it shrinks back again in a few seconds.

If this behaviour suits you, fine; if not, you can force the Notification Area to remain fully expanded.

Now you see them...

and now you don't.

- *Notification Area*
- *Properties*
- *Taskbar tab*
- *uncheck Hide inactive icons*
- *Apply*
- *OK*

Alternatively, you can retain dynamic resizing but specify that certain icons should remain visible at all times. Click the Customize button next to Hide inactive icons and work your way through the list of possibilities. When you click on an item, a dropdown menu appears with three self-explanatory options: Hide when inactive, Always hide and Always show. In this way you can permanently hide utilities that run happily in the background without any intervention while keeping, say, the volume control icon within view.

Keep the Notification Area trim by hiding icons you don't need to monitor.

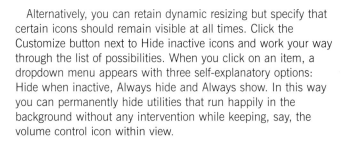

Take control of the Notification Area.

3

PART **3** WINDOWS XP
Exploring Explorer

PART ③ **What's new**

In Windows XP, Explorer gets a dramatic makeover. The main change is the introduction of a task-based approach, by which means Windows endeavours to put the tools you are most likely to require at any given time within easy reach. For instance, when you browse a bunch of folders, it provides fast-track options to rename, move, copy, publish (to the web), share, e-mail and delete folders.

The new Task Pane puts the tools you'll most likely need at your fingertips.

This change in direction is mainly designed to make computing more intuitive for the beginner – and, in our opinion, it succeeds. It certainly should help you get from A to B more quickly, spend less time fiddling with Windows and spend more time doing productive stuff with your computer. Inevitably, though, any enforced change in working style can be irksome to the more experienced Windows user.

Windows Explorer doesn't exactly leap out and grab you from the Start menu but you'll more commonly see it manifested as My Documents and My Computer.

Accessories ▶	Accessibility ▶	
eJay Soundbrowser ▶	Communications ▶	
Games ▶	Entertainment ▶	
Gigabyte EasyTune4 ▶	System Tools ▶	
InControl ▶	Address Book	
Intel Application Accelerator ▶	Calculator	
Internet Cleanup ▶	Command Prompt	
Island Codeworks Internet Backup ▶	Notepad	
Jasc Software ▶	Paint	
Lavasoft Ad-aware ▶	Program Compatibility Wizard	
Lavasoft Ad-aware 6 ▶	Scanner and Camera Wizard	
Logitech ▶	Synchronize	
MasterSplitter ▶	Tour Windows XP	
Microsoft Clip Gallery ▶	Windows Explorer	
Microsoft Encarta ▶	Windows Movie Maker	
Microsoft Works ▶	WordPad	
Norton AntiVirus ▶		
NutriBase SR13 ▶		
Paint Shop Pro 6 ▶		

My Documents

When you open the My Documents folder to work with files (or My Computer to work with hardware) what you get is a Windows Explorer window. You can also access Windows Explorer directly from the Start menu –

Start

All programs

Accessories

Windows Explorer

but in fact this simply takes you to My Documents, too

Titlebar

Address bar

Menu bar

Toolbar *As ever, the Back, Forward and Up A Level buttons aid navigation through a hierarchy of folers*

Tasks view pane *In a major departure from previous versions of Windows, the Tasks view tries to predict your next move and put the requisite tool at your fingertips. The contents of this panel vary according to the type of folder currently being viewed*

Other places *Again, Windows has a stab at guessing where you might want to go to next and provides a few likely-looking links*

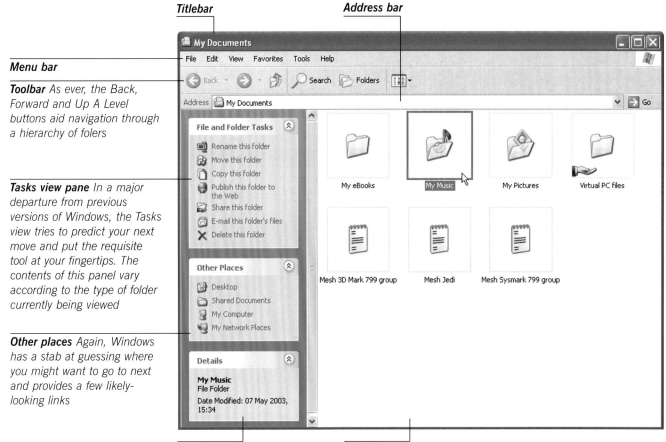

Details *Point at any file or folder in the main window and here you see a few descriptive details. Note that all of these panes can be 'rolled up' (minimised) by clicking the double chevron symbol*

Main window

Moving My Documents

My Documents is the default top-level folder for user-created files. Most Windows programs take it for granted that you will save your files there, and some even create their own sub-folders there in readiness: My Pineapple Projects, My SwankySoft Files, and so on.

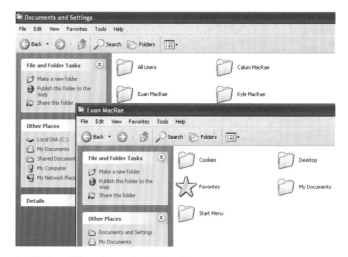

Many programs plant their own sub-folders within My Documents during installation on the assumption that this is where you'll save your files. Indeed, the Save As dialogue box will probably point right to this folder.

You are, of course, free to save files in any other folder whatsoever but it makes good sense to use My Documents if for no other reason than it makes backing up everything at one fell swoop that much easier. Shortcuts to My Documents also appear just about everywhere in Windows XP so it requires a measure of persistence to shun it.

The default location of My Documents is C:\Documents and Settings\User Name\My Documents (where C: is the hard disk or disk partition that contains Windows). The User Name part of the path is important because every User Account holder has his own My Documents folder. That is, when user Jack clicks on My Documents, he uses C:\Documents and Settings\Jack\My Documents; when user Jill logs on, she sees C:\Documents and Settings\Jill\My Documents, and so forth.

In Windows XP, each user has his or her own My Documents folder. To see the full collection, browse to C:\Documents and

These folders are quite distinct and semi-private. We work with User Accounts in detail in Part Five.

However, you can change the location of My Documents. You might, for instance, wish to keep your files on a separate disk partition that can be backed up daily in its entirety. The procedure for moving My Documents is not obvious – don't try dragging and dropping the folder; it won't work – but it is straightforward.

- Start
- My Documents icon
- Properties
- Move

  Select a new location
- OK
- Apply
- OK

  Once relocated, you can carry on working with the My Documents folder as normal; existing documents are transferred, Explorer shortcuts function just as before and the change in location is transparent.

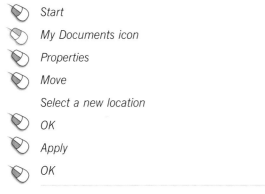

When you move My Documents, existing files are transported to the new location.

Making shortcuts

Windows XP trips over itself to provide ubiquitous shortcuts to My Documents, including one in the Tasks View pane in every Explorer window. My Documents is thus itself a useful repository for shortcuts to other frequently-accessed folders.

- Start
- My Documents icon
- any clear spot within the main window
- New
- Shortcut
- Browse

  Select the folder you wish to target
- OK
- Next
- Finish

  You can rename the shortcut at this point or accept the suggested name (which echoes the name of the folder). If you create a lot of shortcuts in My Documents, you might wish to keep things tidy by storing them all within a single sub-folder called, perhaps, My Shortcuts.

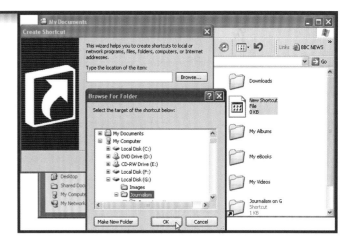

Create shortcuts to frequently-used folders in My Documents for easy access from anywhere within Windows.

Tasks View and Explorer Bars

The Tasks View pane changes appearance according to the type of files currently being viewed in the Explorer window.

Open My Documents or My Computer – i.e. launch Windows Explorer in either folders or drives mode – and note the split screen. To the right are items, folders, files and drives; to the left is the Tasks View pane. The top section of this pane – File and Folder Tasks – changes appearance dynamically in tune with your actions and the types of file you are currently working with.

If you open a folder containing music files, for instance, the Tasks View pane invites you to play them, create an audio CD or, rather tenuously, shop for music online (Microsoft has partner agreements with several web-based retailers). If you select a folder full of images, you can view them as a slide show, print them, burn them to CD or, equally tenuously, order hard copy prints online (Microsoft also has partner agreements with several photo developers).

The middle section of the Tasks View pane – Other Places – provides shortcuts to key folders; and the lower section – Details – provides information about any file selected in the main pane. What's more, image files are automatically previewed in thumbnail mode.

Image files in any folder can be previewed in the Tasks View pane. Click the chevrons to minimise File and Folder Tasks and Other Places.

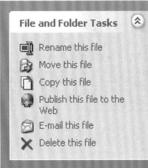

QUICK Q & A

How do I know whether I'm copying or moving a file when I drag and drop it from A to B.
If you use the left mouse button for dragging, Windows XP automatically moves a file if the destination is on the same hard disk as the source, and copies it if the source and destination are on separate disks or drives. Or is it the other way around? We can

never remember, which is why it is safer to use the right mouse button for dragging. Just select Copy Here or Move Here from the popup menu when dropping.

Copy Here
Move Here
Create Shortcuts Here

Cancel

This tools-at-your-fingertips twist is at the very heart of Windows XP, but is it useful? Well, yes and no, in our opinion, depending on how familiar you are with, and wedded to, right-clicking. That is, the Tasks View pane largely duplicates the context-sensitive right-click mouse menu, and does so at the expense of available screen space. If you would rather stick with clicks, you can lose Task View completely or switch it off temporarily.

To be done with it once and for all, open My Documents and

- *Tools*
- *Folder Options…*
- *General tab*
- *Use Windows classic folders*
- *Apply*
- *OK*

All Explorer windows will now open as single-screen windows.

To disable the Tasks View pane temporarily, click the Folders button on the toolbar. This replaces the Tasks View pane with a Folders View pane that displays a 'traditional' view of files and folders on your hard disk.

Switching to Classic mode expels the Tasks View pane.

Choose your poison: Explorer windows with or without Folders View.

Even if you turn off the Tasks View feature completely, you can still have a Folders View pane in Explorer. Click the Folders button to toggle between split-screen and single-screen windows.

Toggle between the Tasks View and Folders View panes with the toolbar button. The Folders View pane has a close button in the top-right corner; click this and Explorer reverts to the Tasks View pane.

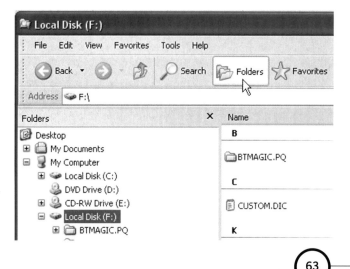

Explorer Bars

The Folders View pane mentioned above is but one of five Explorer bars that can replace the Tasks View pane on demand.

 Open any Explorer window

 View

 Explorer Bar and make a selection

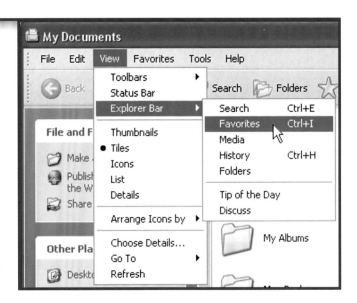

Toggle between the Tasks View and Folders View panes with the toolbar button. The Folders View pane has a close button in the top-right corner; click this and Explorer reverts to the Tasks View pane.

But what do they all do?

- **Search** Opens the Window Search Assistant utility for finding files. Search can also be accessed via a link in the Start menu.

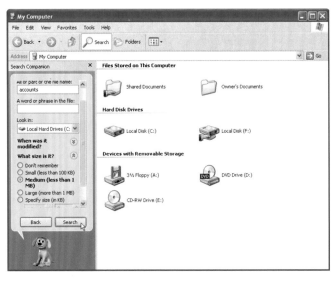

Dumb dog aside, the Search tool is one way to track down elusive files.

- **Favorites** Displays your Favorites folder. This folder is home to internet bookmarks but it can also hold shortcuts to standard files and folders. To add a shortcut, open My Documents, enable the Favorites Explorer Bar, and navigate to the target item in the main window. Now drag it across to Favorites with the right mouse button and select Create Shortcut Here when you drop it in place.

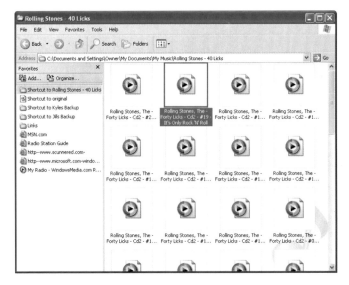

Keep your bookmarks and frequently-accessed folders a click away with Favorites.

● **Media** Just a link to the WindowsMedia.com website, and generally best ignored.

Streaming music and video over the internet ... and a steady sales pitch from Microsoft.

● **History** A clickable index of recently-viewed web pages and recently-opened files. If you click a link to a document, it opens in its host application; click a web page and Explorer transforms into Internet Explorer (more or less). You can work with the History index in several ways; click the View and Search buttons at the top of the Bar to experiment. To clear History and start afresh,

- *open Internet Explorer*
- *Tools*
- *internet Options*
- *General tab*
- *Clear History*

Backtrack to any earlier file or web page in Explorer with the History bar.

● **Folders** An expandable tree-like hierarchical index of files and folders, very useful for navigation.

Frill-free navigation with the Folders View.

Add toolbar buttons

With the exception of Media, you can add shortcuts to Explorer Bars on the main Explorer toolbar. Annoyingly, Explorer bar selections are lost when you close the window and must be reopened afresh each time. Toolbar buttons re-enable Explorer Bars with a quick click.

In fact, Folders and Search buttons should already be present on the Standard Buttons toolbar. To add the others,

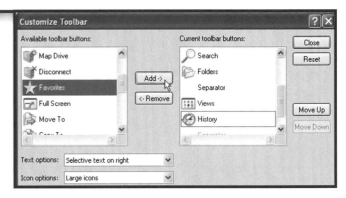

Plant a convenient button on the toolbar for each Explorer Bar you use regularly.

- 🖱 *the toolbar in any Explorer window*
- 🖱 *Customize*
- 🖱 *Select options in the Available toolbar buttons section*
- 🖱 *Add*

There are some other options in there that might take your fancy, too. Use the Move up and Move down buttons to rearrange the position of buttons on the toolbar.

Adding toolbars

In addition to the Standard Buttons toolbar that is essential for navigation and provides some useful shortcuts, Explorer windows can be adorned with a couple of optional toolbars borrowed from the Taskbar: the Address Bar, for launching web content (p51); and Links, with which you can open any file, folder or item straight from an Explorer window (p51). Together, they offer yet another alternative to the Desktop, Start menu or Taskbar.

Open an Explorer window – My Documents or any other folder – then right-click either the menu bar or button toolbar and check Address Bar or Links or both. Once enabled, these new toolbars can be dragged into new dimensions, locked in place, given a row each or forced to share space. Any changes you make in one Explorer window (like My Documents) are remembered and carried through to all other Explorer windows (like My Computer).

You cannot, however, add custom toolbars to Explorer as you can with the Taskbar.

Explorer toolbars can be arranged pretty much anyhow: one row for each, squeezed together, and left locked or unlocked.

Simple Folder View

One nice new feature in Explorer is the oddly-named Simple Folder View. You might not notice the difference at first but here's how it works.

Open My Documents or any other Explorer window and click the Folders button to enable Folders View. In this pane, find any folder icon with a little + sign next to it. This designates a top-level folder containing sub-folders. Now click the folder icon (not the + sign). As you might expect, the contents of the folder appear in the main Explorer window. The folder itself also expands in the Folders View pane to reveal the first level of sub-folders.

Now click a different top-level folder in the Folders View pane. Again, the folder expands by one level and its contents appear in the right pane. However, the first folder that you expanded simultaneously contracts. This is a seemingly small detail but it has the effect that only one top-level folder is expanded in the Folders View pane at any time.

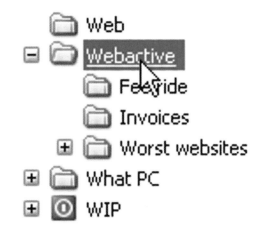

By default, only one top-level folder is shown expanded in Folders View; expand a second folder and the first one contracts.

In earlier versions of Windows, you had to double-click a folder to get it to expand in the first place; and then it stayed expanded even when you moved away and double-clicked others. The outcome could be a long, unwieldy hierarchy. However, if this auto-contraction behaviour bugs you, you can force folders to remain expanded in the Folders View pane by clicking the plus symbol instead of the folder icon. And if it really, really bugs you, you can turn off Simple Folder View altogether.

Open an Explorer window

Tools button

Folder Options

View tab

Display simple folder view in Explorer's Folders list

Apply

OK

New views

The spruced-up and revamped Explorer interface also lets
you view and work with files in interesting new ways.
The following options can all be turned on by clicking the
Views toolbar button in any Explorer window or through
the View menu.

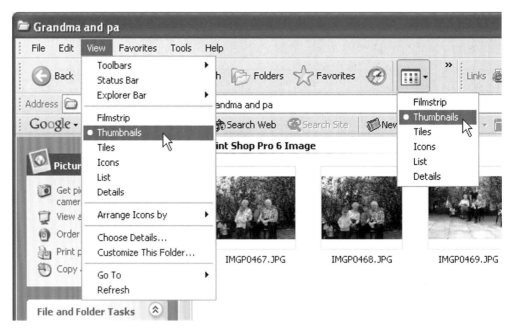

*Two ways to experiment with
Explorer views: the View menu
and the Views button.*

● **Thumbnails** Small graphical representations of files,
particularly useful for browsing images and saved web pages
(HTML files). In Thumbnails view, folder icons display mini-
thumbnails of image files held within.

● **Icons** Each file is represented by an icon related to its host
application.

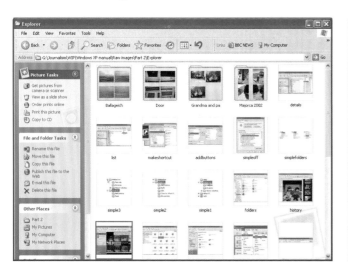

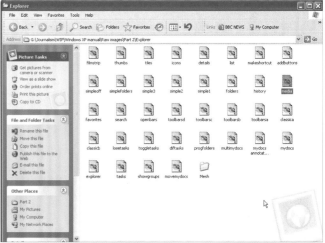

● **Tiles** Bigger icons, basically. Each tile is accompanied by three lines of descriptive text, including the file size.

● **List** A simple, spare list of files.

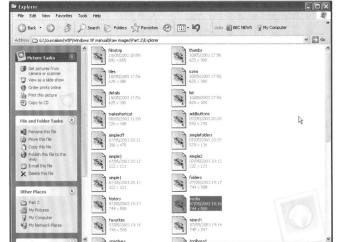

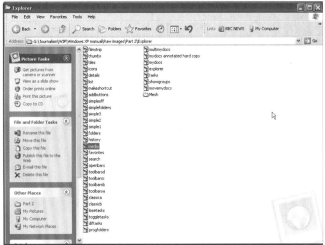

● **Details** Probably the most useful view. Here, you get to see as much or as little information about files as you choose. By default, Explorer includes columns for file name, size, type and date modified but you can right-click any column heading and add extra columns from the popup menu.

● **Filmstrip** This one is useful for folders that contain lots of image files. Click once on any image and it is displayed in a large preview window. Simple navigational controls let you scroll through subsequent images. With the Tasks View pane open, click View as a slide show to see your images displayed sequentially in full-screen mode.

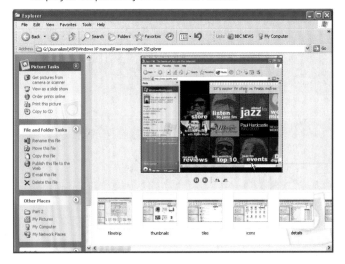

Global settings

When you find an Explorer view that you like, it is straightforward to apply it to all folders. Open any Explorer window and apply the view of your choice.

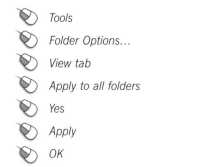

- Tools
- Folder Options…
- View tab
- Apply to all folders
- Yes
- Apply
- OK

All Explorer windows will now open with the same view.

However, you can override the default setting for specific folders. Let's say you have one folder full of digital images that you would rather work with in Filmstrip view. Simply open that folder in Explorer and change the view. Explorer will remember your settings and always apply them when you return to this particular folder, but all other folders retain the global default setting.

One view suits all? Apply it to every folder in one move.

Organise folders

When you have folders full of sub-folders or crammed with dozens or even hundreds of files, it helps to have some additional way of organising them. Open such a folder in an Explorer window, right-click anywhere in the main window and point at the Arrange Icons By menu option. This lets you organise the contents of the folder by file name, size, type or when files were last modified or opened.

That's fine as far as it goes. However, you can also check the Show in Groups option from the same right-click menu to persuade Explorer to shuffle files into further order. Each folder can be customised individually or you can apply a preference globally (see Global settings above). Note that the Show in Groups feature works whichever view is selected except Thumbnails and, curiously, List.

▲ *Auto-arrange your folder icons.* ▼ *For easier navigation, let Explorer group your files and folders.*

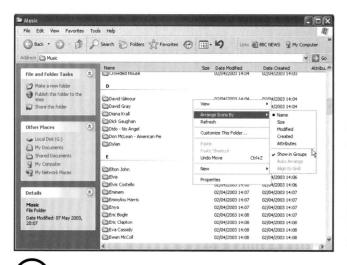

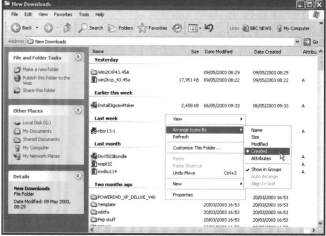

Folder templates

For still further customisation, Windows XP provides a selection of folder templates. These work best when you keep similar files together e.g. use one folder for music files, another for images, another for documents and so forth. To be honest, we've only found templates useful for image and music folders – and the My Pictures and My Music sub-folders in My Documents are best suited to these files in any case – but a little experimentation may pay dividends. Note that the old 'folder background' feature has vanished with XP i.e. you can no longer use an image file as the backdrop to an Explorer window.

To apply or tweak a template,

- *open any folder*
- *anywhere in the main pane*
- *Customize This Folder…*
- *Customize tab*

  In the Use this folder type as a template section, choose the option that best describes the files in the folder.

- *If you like, check Also apply this template to all subfolders to apply the settings to the entire contents of the folder.*
- *Apply*
- *OK*

Folder templates work best when you keep files of the same type together. The associated Tasks View pane then provides shortcuts suited to that template/those files.

Pictures on folders

When a folder contains image files, Windows plants four thumbnails on the folder icon to remind you of what's inside. This only works in Thumbnails view, mind: switch to Tiles, Icons or any other view and image-adorned folders become as buff and boring as any other.

If you prefer, you can specify that a single picture should adorn a given folder. This can be any image from within the folder or elsewhere.

One image per folder, or four: your choice.

- *the folder icon in an Explorer window*
- *Properties*
- *Customize tab*
- *Choose Picture. Now browse to an image*
- *Open*
- *Apply*
- *OK*

Alternatively, simply rename any image within the folder folder.jpg and it will automatically be displayed on the folder icon.

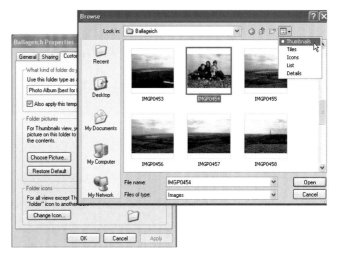

Use Thumbnails view in the Browse window to help you find a suitable image for a folder icon.

Change folder icons

Alternatively, instead of pasting pictures on folders, you can change folder icons to pictures. This is one way of locating key folders at a glance from a sea of clones and has the advantage that the effect shows up in all views, not just Thumbnails. Right-click any folder and follow the steps in the previous section to open the Customize tab. Now click Change Icon and select one of the proffered icons. If you want to use one of your own images as an icon, use an image editor to resize it to 32 x 32 pixels and save it in bitmap format.

You can use any image as a folder icon so long as it has a .BMP extension. When browsing, select All Files in the Files of type box or else Windows will look only for known icon files (which have an .ICO extension).

Renaming files

You can rename a group of files in one hit with Windows XP. Open a folder in an Explorer window and select your target files (hold down the Control key to select multiple files simultaneously). Now right-click any file in the group, select Rename from the popup menu, type a new file name and hit Enter. The image that you right-clicked acquires the new name – let's say Park Pictures – and all other selected images become Park Pictures(1), Park Pictures(2), and so on. To undo changes on a file-by-file basis, click the Edit menu and select Undo Rename.

Note that if Explorer is configured to hide file extensions, you will have to include the correct extension when specifying the file name e.g. Park Pictures.jpg. It is easier to make file extensions visible first (see p75).

Rename files en masse from the right-click menu.

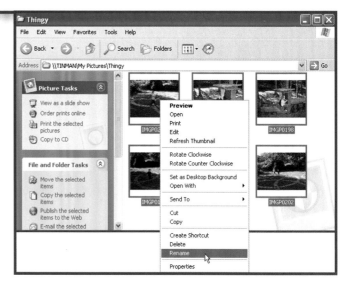

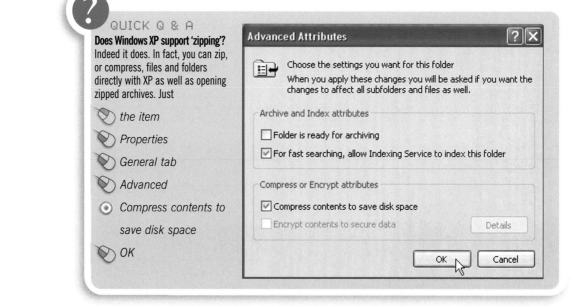

QUICK Q & A

Does Windows XP support 'zipping'?
Indeed it does. In fact, you can zip, or compress, files and folders directly with XP as well as opening zipped archives. Just

- *the item*
- *Properties*
- *General tab*
- *Advanced*
- *Compress contents to save disk space*
- *OK*

Folder Options

For more advanced options that go beyond the mere prettification of folders, click Tools on the menu toolbar in any Explorer window, followed by Folder Options. There are three tabs here, each of which lets you control certain aspects of Explorer's – and thus Windows XP's – overall deportment.

Let's consider these in turn.

General tab

There are only three options in here:

- **Tasks** As discussed on p63, this toggles the Tasks View pane on and off.

- **Browse folders** If you want Windows to spawn a new Explorer window every time you open a folder, change the default option here; otherwise, new folders open within the same window. You can always navigate between folders with the Back, Forward and Up buttons on the standard toolbar.

- **Click items as follows** A purely personal preference. By default, Windows XP requires double-clicking to open files and folders but you can make it more internet-like by switching to single clicks throughout. If you've never tried single-clicking, give it a whirl for a while.

View tab

The View tab takes us into deeper but more fruitful territory.

- **Automatically search for network folders and printers** If you are connected to a network, this useful option makes Windows look for recent changes, including the addition of shared folders and printers. If found, they are automatically added to your My Network Places folder (see p107).

- **Display file size information in folder tips** Simpler than it sounds: with this turned on, you can hover your mouse over any folder icon in an Explorer window and be rewarded with an informative popup bubble.

- **Display the contents of system folders** Check this option to stop Windows hiding critical files that it needs to operate (including the entire contents of the Windows folder). Leave it unchecked unless you really need to root around in system folders.

- **Display simple folder view in Explorer's Folder list** See p67 above.

Set a few global preferences here.

File Folder

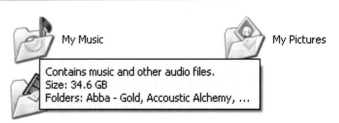

Keep tabs on folder size and contents with tips-in-a-bubble.

- **Display the full path in the address bar** Useful if and only if you equip your Explorer windows with an Address toolbar (p66). Check this box and it displays the full system or network location of the current item (e.g. C:\Documents and Settings\Kyle\My Documents\My eBooks\Harry Potter Collection\Goblet\Chapter One). Unchecked, the Address bar displays only the file or folder name.

- **Display the full path in the title bar** As above, except this time the change affects an Explorer window's Title Bar. For our money, displaying the full path merely adds unnecessary clutter to the window.

- **Do not cache thumbnails** This affects the way in which Windows works with thumbnails. Unchecked, it plucks images from a cache to save time and effort; checked, it redraws every image afresh whenever you view thumbnails in an Explorer window. The default cached option is usually fine.

- **Hidden files and folders** Unless you say otherwise, files and folders that Windows decrees should be hidden do not appear in Explorer windows. This helps prevent accidents but there may be times when you need to access hidden files (see p93, for example). Disable file hiding here as and when required.

Display the full path to any file in the Address Bar (turned on here) or Title bar (turned off here), or both, or neither.

When viewed in Explorer, hidden files have semi-transparent icons. Generally, it is safer to keep them completely out of sight and harm's way.

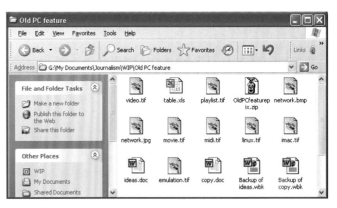

Visible file extensions help you tell one file type from another, especially when different formats are associated with the same program and thus share the same icon.

- **Hide extensions for known file types** When Explorer recognises a file type – a Word document, for instance – it displays only the document name and ignores the extension (e.g. LetterToMum rather than LetterToMum.doc). In most cases, that is fine. However, there are times when it helps to have the extension visible, such as when renaming files (p72) or associating files of a given type with a particular application (p77).

- **Hide protected operating system files** Short of serious system surgery, you should leave this option checked.

- **Launch folder windows in a separate process** A roundabout way of making Windows use extra memory every time it opens a new window. One to ignore and leave unchecked.

- **Managing pairs of web pages and folders** When you save or create a web page, the result is typically an HTML file plus an associated folder containing the multimedia elements used in the page. This option ensures that when you move, copy or delete the HTML file, the associated folder is automatically moved, copied or deleted too.

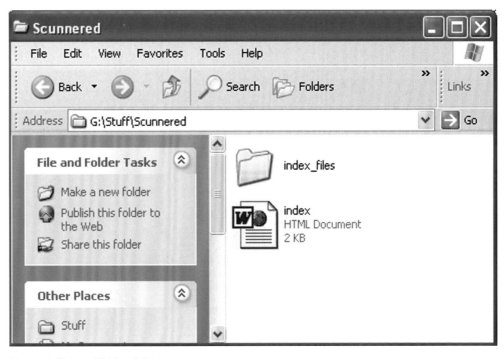

Keep web files and folders linked for easy management of web projects.

- **Remember each folder's view settings** If you uncheck this option, any view settings you tweak for a particular folder are forgotten next time you open it. Usually, that would rather defeat the purpose of making the change in the first place. However, if you prefer to maintain a uniform appearance across your folders, this option lets you temporarily change view settings without lasting effect.

- **Restore previous Windows folders at log on** It is possible to log off Windows without closing open Explorer windows. Check this option if you make a habit of this and would like the same windows to automatically reopen next time you log on (as used to happen automatically in earlier versions of Windows).

- **Show Control Panel in My Computer** As it says, if you would like an icon for Control Panel in the My Computer folder, check the box. We prefer the tweak discussed on p50, although they are not exclusive.

- **Show encrypted or compressed NTFS files in color** If you compress a folder in Windows XP (see p72), its file name and any additional information shown in Details view are given a blue font in Explorer; encrypt it (see p16), and the font turns green.

- **Show popup description for folder and desktop items** It seems that every time you point at anything in Windows XP, up pops a little bubble with explanatory text. Useful or intrusive, you decide – and turn the feature off or on here.

Spot a compressed folder at 40 paces with coloured text in Explorer views.

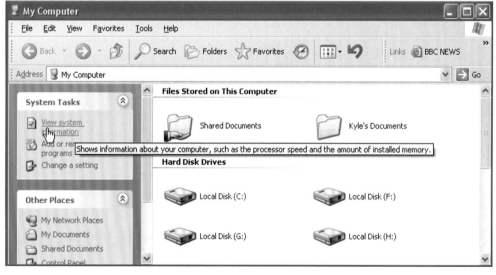

Popup bubbles tell you what something is or does before you click it but they can get in the way.

File Types tab

Finally, the File Types tab tells you what kind of files are currently on your computer and which applications are associated with them. Although you may have several programs installed that are capable of playing an MP3 music file, say, or editing a JPG image, only one application is ever the default application for a given file type i.e. the program that opens automatically when you open the file.

Some programs are notorious for 'stealing' file associations and overriding earlier settings; here, in the Opens With section, you can reclaim your preferences. Select the file type by its extension in the main window, click the Change button and either select one of the Recommended Programs or use the Other Programs list to specify an alternative. If your program of choice is not listed, use the Browse button to navigate to the relevant executable file (usually found in C:\Progam Files).

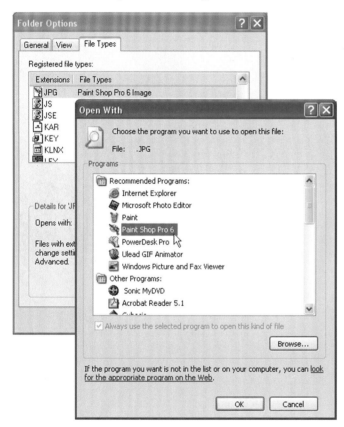

Specify which programs are associated with specific file types.

And if it all goes wrong...

Mastering Explorer is the lynchpin of a successful XP survival strategy but, for all the new flexibility of the Windows Explorer, there is no single set of settings that will suit everybody. You might prefer the stark but informative Details view or you may enjoy customising folders in many different ways. If at any time you get in a muddle with views, pictures on folders, customised icons and template (as we do, frequently), just reset all folders to their default settings and start again. Click Tools on the menu toolbar in any Explorer window, then click Folder Options. Open the View tab and click the Reset All Folders button.

QUICK Q & A

How can I stop Windows asking me what I want to do every time I put a CD or DVD in a drive?

Irritating, isn't it, when a popup window asks whether you want to play audio files, watch video clips, print pictures and so? To modify this behaviour, open My Computer and right-click your CD or DVD drive icon. Select Properties and open the AutoPlay tab. Here you can set the default Windows action for discs that contain particular file types. You might, for instance, want DVD movies and audio CDs to play automatically but prefer that Windows should ignore data discs. Select each file type from the drop-down menu, check Select an action to perform and make your choices here. Uncheck the Prompt me each time to choose an action box to make your choices permanent.

PART **4** WINDOWS XP
Connections

Making an internet connection

If you perform an over-the-top upgrade to Windows XP or use the Files and Settings Transfer Wizard, your existing internet settings should be preserved. Failing that, or when you need to set up a new connection, you will have to configure your computer to dial an Internet Service Provider (ISP). Nothing too radical is required: XP provides a wizard. This replaces the Make New Connection wizard, just as Network Connections replaces the Dial-Up Networking folder of old.

New Connection Wizard
To configure a connection to your ISP, follow this procedure. Before starting, make sure that you have your ISP account details, including your user name, password and the telephone number provided for internet access. Oh, and a modem installed in your computer.

Start

Control Panel

Network and Internet connections

Set up or change your Internet connection

Connections tab

Setup

This launches the New Connection Wizard.

Internet Properties

General | Security | Privacy | Content | Connections | Programs | Advanced

To set up an Internet connection, click Setup. [Setup...]

Dial-up and Virtual Private Network settings

[Add...] [Remove]

Choose Settings if you need to configure a proxy server for a connection. [Settings...]

⦿ Never dial a connection
○ Dial whenever a network connection is not present
○ Always dial my default connection

Current   None   [Set Default]

Local Area Network (LAN) settings

LAN Settings do not apply to dial-up connections. Choose Settings above for dial-up settings. [LAN Settings...]

[OK] [Cancel] [Apply]

②

Next

Connect to the Internet

Next

You can also use the wizard to set up a local network – as we will on p85 – but here we are concerned with the wider world.

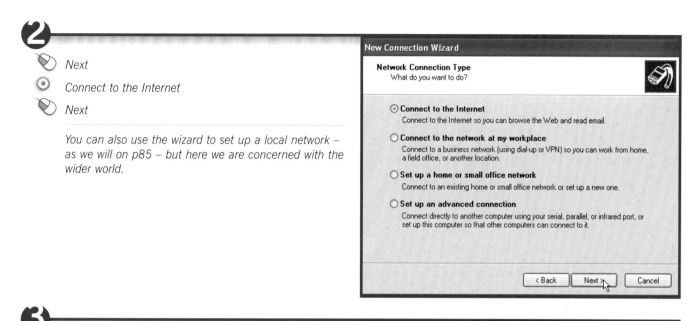

③

Set up my connection manually

Next

Forget any notion of using an automated process – it just doesn't work.

④

Connect using a dial-up modem

Next

We will assume here that your computer uses a standard analogue modem. Contrary to appearances, you should also use this setting for a broadband internet service if your ISP supplied you with a DSL or cable modem that connects to the computer via a USB port (as does BT Openworld, for one). If you have more than one device installed – an internal analogue modem and an external DSL broadband modem, for instance – the wizard asks you to specify which device should be used for this connection.

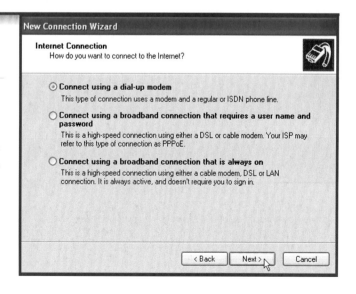

5

⌨ ISP name   ⌨ Your ISP user name

🖱 Next   ⌨ Your ISP password

⌨ Telephone number   ⌨ Confirm password

🖱 Next   ⦿ All options

                                       🖱 Next

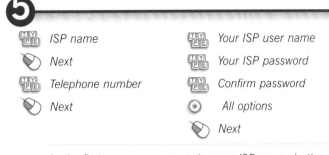

In the first screen you see, enter your ISP name; in the second, enter the telephone number that you use to connect to your ISP. Note that if you subscribe to a broadband internet service, you can leave the telephone number field blank. Finally, type in your ISP user name and password. Leave the three options in the lower part of the window checked (see Quick Q & A on p83).

6

🖱 Finish

You can ask for a Desktop shortcut, if you like. The wizard now concludes and the connection is ready for testing.

7

🖱 Start

🖱 Connect To

🖱 New internet connection

🖱 Dial

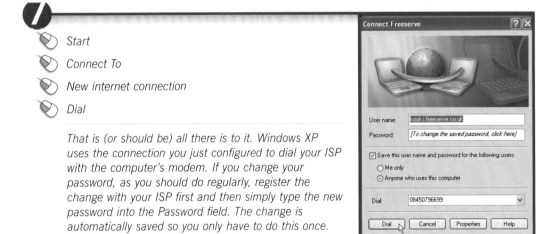

That is (or should be) all there is to it. Windows XP uses the connection you just configured to dial your ISP with the computer's modem. If you change your password, as you should do regularly, register the change with your ISP first and then simply type the new password into the Password field. The change is automatically saved so you only have to do this once.

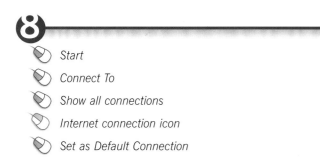

8

- Start
- Connect To
- Show all connections
- Internet connection icon
- Set as Default Connection

This opens the Network Connections folder (more usually accessed from My Network Places – see p85), wherein you can view and modify all network settings, including internet and local network connections. Right-click your new connection and make it the default internet connection.

9

- Start
- Control Panel
- Network and Internet Connections
- internet Options
- Connections tab
- Always dial my default connection

This final step ensures that Windows knows to use this connection to connect to the internet on demand e.g. whenever you send an e-mail or open a web page in Internet Explorer.

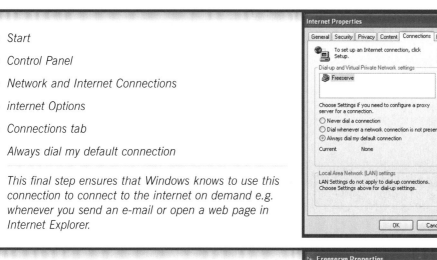

10

Repeat Step 8 but select Properties from the right-click popup menu. This is where you can modify settings if required. Open the Advanced tab to check that the firewall is enabled (as it should be if you left the option checked in Step 5). You can also manually configure internet connection settings here but in our experience there is seldom, if ever, the need to play around. In fact, should a connection start malfunctioning, it is usually easier to delete it in My Network Places and run the wizard afresh.

QUICK Q & A

Is the Windows XP firewall all I need?
That depends on how carefully you prevent malicious software from installing on your computer. The XP firewall effectively makes your computer invisible on the internet, so potential hackers can neither sense its presence nor find a way in. However, the firewall does not stop programs, including worms and spyware, finding a way out from your computer to

the internet at large. It is a one-way thing, in short; no bugs or attacks can get through but you have no control over what goes out. Commercial firewalls usually offer two-way control and alert you every time a program or process attempts to make an internet connection. Remember too that there is no protection against viruses in Windows so you will certainly need a third-party anti-virus product.

Internet Connection Firewall

☑ Protect my computer and network by limiting or preventing access to this computer from the Internet

Learn more about Internet Connection Firewall.

PART 4 Setting up a home network

Networking is all about sharing, of course: sharing an internet connection, sharing files and folders, sharing hardware devices. The moment you have two or more computers at home or at work, it makes sense to network them – and here again Windows XP scores serious ease-of-use points.

In this worked example, we will run the Network Setup Wizard and enable internet Connection Sharing. When configuring a network, always begin with the computer that has the direct connection to the internet.

When you run the Network Setup Wizard on subsequent computers, it automatically detects a shared internet connection.

Network Setup Wizard

Do you want to use the shared connection?

The wizard found a shared Internet connection on the computer "TINMAN."

Do you want to use the existing shared connection for this computer's Internet access?

⦿ Yes, use the existing shared connection for this computer's Internet access (recommended)

◯ No, let me choose another way to connect to the Internet

< Back   Next >   Cancel

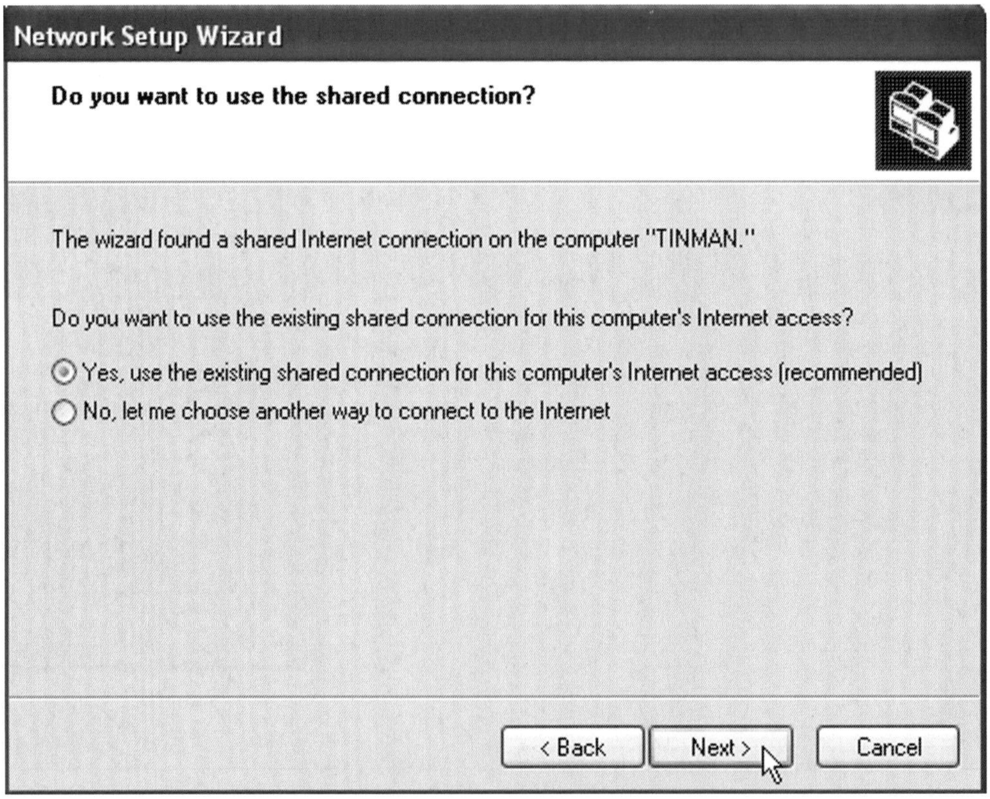

What hardware do I need for networking?

Generally speaking, you need an Ethernet network interface card (NIC) in each computer, a hub or switch between them, and Category 5 cables to make the connections. You can buy network-in-a-box kits that simplify everything: see, for instance www.netgear.com, www.linksys.com and www.belkin.com. So long as one computer on the network has direct access to the internet – i.e. a modem connected to a telephone line or broadband service – all others can share its connection. A router is an optional accessory whereby a separate hardware device manages the internet connection and filters traffic through the network. This usually works just fine with Windows XP, particularly if the router supports the UPnP (Universal Plug and Play) standard. Wireless networking – WiFi – is a network without cables. Again, this is supported by XP and should 'just work'.

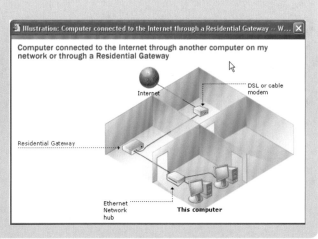

Start

Control Panel

Network and Internet Connections

Set up or change your home or small office network

This launches the Network Setup Wizard.

Next

Next

Select the appropriate option

Next

Select the first option here because this computer connects directly to the internet. When running the wizard on your other computers subsequently, check the second option. Note that a 'residential gateway' is typically a hardware router that connects directly to a broadband internet connection. All networked computers then connect directly or indirectly to this device – i.e. none has a direct modem connection to the internet – so the second option would be appropriate.

3

○ *Select your Internet connection*

🖱 *Next*

Select your internet connection from the list. This is the connection you set up with the internet Connection Wizard, and will be named according to your choice in Step 5 on p82.

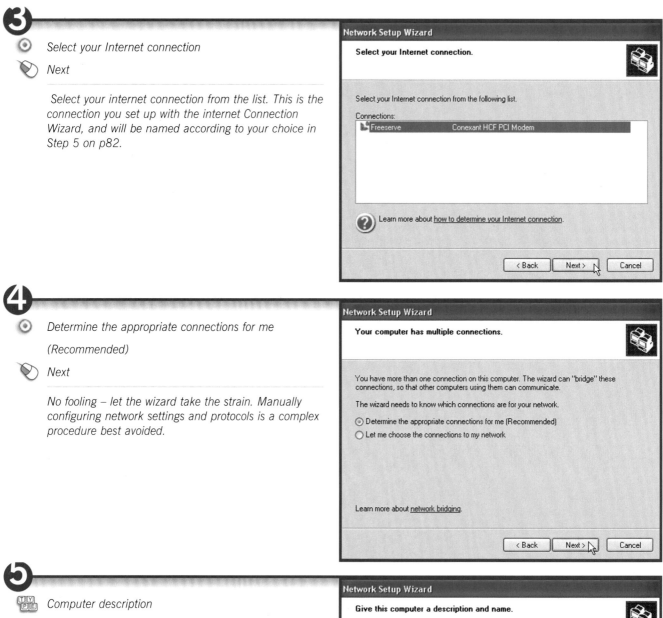

4

○ *Determine the appropriate connections for me*

(Recommended)

🖱 *Next*

No fooling – let the wizard take the strain. Manually configuring network settings and protocols is a complex procedure best avoided.

5

⌨ *Computer description*

⌨ *Computer name*

🖱 *Next*

The descriptive field is useful for easy identification of computers on a network so enter whatever you like. More importantly, each networked computer must have a unique computer name. During installation of XP, you may have given your computer a name or accepted the default (see Step 9 on p27). Either way, this is what you see now. Feel free to change it.

6

Change name if desired

Next

You must give your network a workgroup name. Windows always suggests MSHOME, which is fine. Change it if you like but remember to enter the new workgroup name when you run this wizard on your other computers.

Network Setup Wizard

Name your network.

Name your network by specifying a workgroup name below. All computers on your network should have the same workgroup name.

Workgroup name: `MSHOME`

Examples: HOME or OFFICE

`< Back`   `Next >`   `Cancel`

7

Next

The wizard displays a summary of the network settings and busies itself with internal configuration tasks (which is nice because it means you don't have to). Allow it to finish.

Network Setup Wizard

Ready to apply network settings...

The wizard will apply the following settings. This process may take a few minutes to complete and cannot be interrupted.

Settings:

Internet connection settings:

Internet connection:	Freeserve
Internet connection sharing:	enabled
Internet Connection Firewall:	enabled

Network settings:

Computer description:	Kyle's PC

To apply these settings, click Next.

`< Back`   `Next >`   `Cancel`

8

Just finish the wizard

Next

Finish

Just to summarise: this computer now has a name, is part of a network, and will share its internet connection with any computer on the same network. If you intend to network computers that are not running Windows XP, choose the Create a Network Setup Disk here. This saves your network settings in wizard form on a floppy disk that you should run on each. If your other computers do have Windows XP installed, just run the Network Setup Wizard on each in turn.

Network Setup Wizard

You're almost done...

You need to run the Network Setup Wizard once on each of the computers on your network. To run the wizard on computers that are not running Windows XP, you can use the Windows XP CD or a Network Setup Disk.

What do you want to do?

○ Create a Network Setup Disk

○ Use the Network Setup Disk I already have

○ Use my Windows XP CD

⦿ Just finish the wizard; I don't need to run the wizard on other computers

`< Back`   `Next >`   `Cancel`

5

PART **5** WINDOWS XP
User Accounts

Overview

It has long been possible for several people to use a single computer more or less independently without impacting upon anybody else. Trouble is, or at least was, that such systems could be bamboozling. Well, Windows XP has radically overhauled its approach to multiple users and left us with a system that is, if not foolproof, at least straightforward and flexible.

What is a User Account?

User Accounts is a system that enables different people to log on to Windows and treat it as their own. Each user has his own 'profile' with which to configure Windows to suit his personal style and preferences. User profiles co-exist on a shared computer but a degree of separation between them ensures that privacy is respected.

Specifically, each user has his own:

- My Documents folder (for file storage)
- Desktop (including customisable wallpaper and themes)
- Favorites folder (for bookmarked web pages)
- Cookies (text files used by websites to identify you on return visits)

Thanks to Fast User Switching, described below, one user can step aside to let another log on to Windows without first having to save work, close programs or take any other precautions. Moreover, with the proper use of limited and administrator accounts, interference between users is minimised. Your kids can play games, manage bookmarks and look after their own e-mail account on a shared family computer without the risk that they might inadvertently delete your valuable files.

All users have access to the same installed software but they can set up and work with programs in their own ways. For instance, each user can configure Outlook Express to manage their own – and only their own – e-mail account, and each can customise program elements like toolbar buttons, shortcuts and the spell-checking dictionary in a word processor.

When the computer restarts or one user logs out and ends his session, Windows returns to the Welcome screen and displays an icon for each user. To log on, a user simply clicks his icon and, optionally, enters his password. In short, multiple users get to work with their 'own' copy of Windows XP despite sharing the same hardware.

When competition is fierce for access to the family computer, set up a separate account for everyone. This is the Windows Welcome screen (although it doesn't actually say 'welcome' at all).

Every user has a folder that contains their very own, relatively private My Documents.

Account types

Not all User Accounts are equal. The two most important types are administrator and limited. Now, if your eyes glaze over at the very thought of administrator accounts – Windows 2000 user, perchance? – do bear with us: in Windows XP, it is all really very straightforward.

An administrator has complete control over all User Accounts but a limited user can only make restricted changes to his own account.

Essentially, an administrator can do anything with the computer: install, uninstall and use any program or hardware device; create, manipulate and delete any files; and set up, manage and delete User Accounts and passwords. A limited user can not uninstall software; may not be able to install it either (depending on the program); can only modify his own profile; and can only view another user's files if they have been explicitly shared. In short, a limited user can tweak and customise the computer, but not break it.

If software refuses to install when a limited user is logged on, Windows XP can grant temporary administrator status as a workaround. This does, however, require knowledge of an administrator's user name and password.

There are some further minor limitations, notably that some programs will only run when an administrator is logged on. This is generally a good thing, especially with software that could seriously modify the computer at system-level.

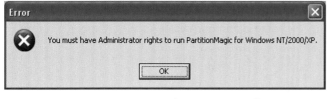

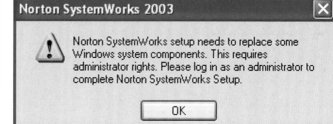

Some programs will only run when an administrator is logged on but most run just fine for limited users.

Not to put too fine a point on it, you don't want the kids repartitioning your hard disk.

A third type of account is the Guest account. This is useful if you need to give somebody temporary access to your computer but a) you don't want to go the full hog and set up a User Account for them, and b) you really, really don't want them poking around your private files and folders. The Guest account has no password protection so anybody can log on to Windows as a Guest from the Welcome screen. That said, the risks are minimal: a Guest can only see files stored in the Shared Documents folder (see p98) and has no access whatsoever to any user's private My Documents folder. The Guest account can only be enabled by an administrator but it is disabled by default and best left that way unless and until you have need of it.

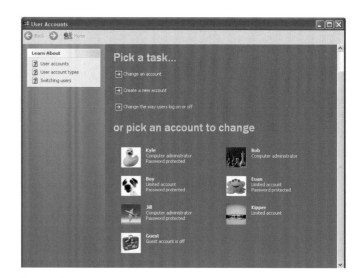

You can have as many User Accounts as you like and choose between them at the Welcome screen, but only grant administrator rights to those that need full control.

Even if you did not set up User Accounts when installing Windows XP (p23), your computer still has one default administrator account. This is usually entitled Owner, although your computer manufacturer may have customised this to ABC Customer, or whatever. When Owner is the only account, it is effectively transparent: when you switch on your computer, Windows takes you straight to the Desktop. However, once you introduce new accounts or add password protection to the default account, the picture changes. Specifically, Windows pauses at the Welcome screen and asks you which account you wish to log on with.

The windows Welcome screen lets users log on to Windows by clicking an icon and entering a password. Click the question mark for your password hint. Where only one User Account exists, normally Owner, this screen is bypassed.

Customising profiles

Aside from administrator or limited status, all new User Accounts start life equal. This is because they are based upon a default user profile that provides each new account with standard features, including the Desktop configuration and a clutch of internet bookmarks. The Default User profile is hidden but it can be customised.

First, ensure that Explorer shows hidden files and folders (see p74). Look in C:\Documents and Settings and there you will find a semi-transparent folder labelled Default User. Inside are, amongst other things, empty Desktop, Favorites and My Documents folders. Any files that you copy to these folders are integrated within the default profile. Thus you might place a couple of essential files in My Documents folder and copy across your existing internet bookmarks to the Favorites folder (or perhaps an edited list tailored for your children). When you next create a User Account, these files and bookmarks will be ready and waiting for the user as soon as they log on.

This is a useful way of pre-configuring User Accounts but it does not affect existing accounts. For that, you need the All Users profile: C:\Documents and Settings\All users. Any administrator can copy items to the Desktop or Start folders here, whereupon they immediately show up – you guessed it – on each user's Desktop and Start menus. Limited users have no access to the All Users profile.

This profile is also home to the Shared Documents folder, which we will look at shortly. There is also a Favorites folder in there but oddly enough it doesn't do very much.

Any files you copy to the Default User profile are incorporated within new User Accounts.

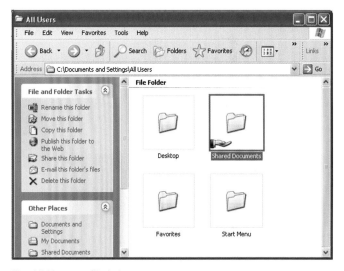

The All Users profile is home to the Shared Documents folder.

QUICK Q & A

Can I uninstall a program when logged on under my User Account without it affecting other users?
No. Only an administrator can uninstall software in the first place, and changes are system-wide i.e. affect all users equally. You can, however, remove program shortcuts from your personal Desktop or Start menu, and disable background processes.

QUICK Q & A

What is a Roaming User profile?
You can save your user profile as a file on a network server. This can then be accessed from any other computer on the network when you log on, with the result that your personal Desktop, Start menu, Favorites and other User Account-specific settings are available to you regardless of where you work. This, however, is really the territory of domain-based company networks with stacks of workstations and flexible seating policies. Furthermore, the computer acting as the network server must be running Windows XP Professional, not Home Edition.

The Administrator account

In the C:\Documents and Settings folder, you may have noticed yet another user profile called Administrator. This is rather confusing. 'The' Administrator is a default, top-level, non-removable User Account quite distinct from a standard administrator account.

In fact, every Windows XP computer has this Administrator account. Normally, you do not – indeed, cannot – log on to Windows as 'the' Administrator because it does not appear as an icon on the Welcome screen. However, in Windows XP Home Edition, press F8 as Windows boots and select Safe Mode. The Administrator icon now temporarily appears on the Welcome screen.

With Windows XP Professional, press Ctrl + Alt + Del twice at the Welcome screen to bring up the Windows 2000-style log on prompt. Type Administrator in the user name field and you can log on without the Safe Mode restrictions.

The Administrator account comes in handy should you ever forget your User Account password (or somehow manage to delete all administrator accounts, which should be impossible – but then according to science bumble-bees can't fly). Log on as Administrator, in Safe Mode if necessary, and reset your password. This is also the only account that can run the Recovery Console (see p159).

The default Administrator password is, remarkably, blank. For more on this all-powerful yet alarmingly insecure account, see p99.

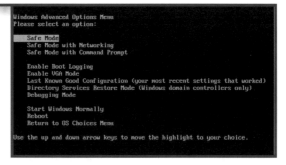

Press F8 during boot to start in Safe Mode and activate the Administrator account on the Welcome screen.

Windows XP Professional prompts you for a secure Administrator password during installation. It is possible, but rather foolish, to leave it blank.

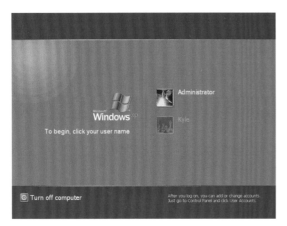

When Administrator appears on the Welcome screen, anybody can log on to a Windows XP computer and have their way with it. The password is, er, blank.

QUICK Q & A

I don't see the Welcome screen when I log on. How do I use 'the' Administrator account?
This could be for a couple of reasons. If you only have one User Account set up, probably the default Owner account, and it is not password-protected, or if you have configured Windows to bypass the Welcome screen in favour of a nominated account (see p101), Windows will log you straight on to the Desktop. This behaviour will continue even in Safe Mode. To access the Welcome screen, either password-protect your default account, even if only temporarily, or ensure that Users must enter a user name and password to use this computer is checked in the User Accounts options screen

⟶ Start

⟶ Run

⌨ control userpasswords2

⟶ OK

Creating a new User Account

Setting up and modifying User Accounts in Windows XP is a breeze. Here we will set up a new account from scratch.

1

- Start
- Control Panel
- User Accounts
- Create a new account

Note the Guest Account option. Click the icon only if you want to turn it on i.e. allow anybody to log in to your computer from the Welcome screen without a password. Otherwise, proceed.

2

- Give the new account a name
- Next
- Make your choice between an administrator and limited account here
- Create Account

That's really all there is to it: Windows XP now allocates a cheesy icon to the account. However, there are plenty of options to tweak.

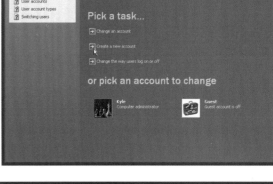

3

- Home
- Click a User Account icon (Kipper, in this case)
- Create a password
- Type in a password twice and include a hint lest you forget it

You can let users create their own passwords if you like. In practice, though, this is largely irrelevant, as any administrator can change any user's password at any time (see below).

Other options here are self-explanatory: change a user name, picture, password or account type (i.e. upgrade a limited account to administrator or downgrade the latter).

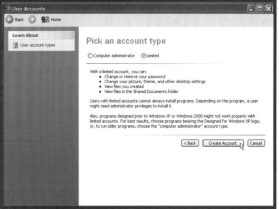
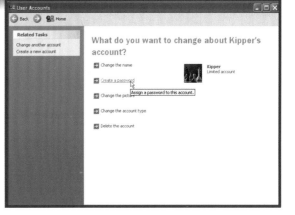

❹

Home

Change the way users log on and off

Use the Welcome screen

Use Fast User Switching

Apply Options

When you're through with passwords, return to the main User Accounts screen and make sure that the Welcome screen and Fast User Switching options are both checked (they should be by default). If you turn off the Welcome screen, you have to type your name and password Windows 2000-style every time you log on instead of clicking an icon. This is a little more secure because user names are hidden but, well, life is short.

❺

Home

Delete the account

Keep Files

Delete

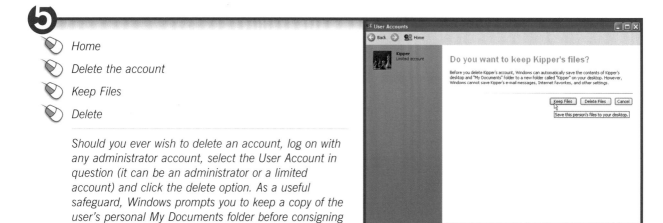

Should you ever wish to delete an account, log on with any administrator account, select the User Account in question (it can be an administrator or a limited account) and click the delete option. As a useful safeguard, Windows prompts you to keep a copy of the user's personal My Documents folder before consigning the account to oblivion. Its contents, if any, are then transferred to a folder on the current user's Desktop.

❻

Start

Log Off

Log Off

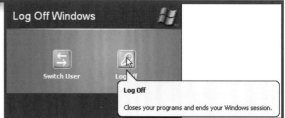

Finally, log off Windows without turning off or restarting the computer (close programs and save files first). This may be the first time you've done this but the button is right there on the Start menu. This terminates your current Windows session without killing the power. The Welcome screen then appears and you or any other account holder can log on afresh.

Fast User Switching

The drawback with logging on and off is that you have to save any open files first. In fact, Windows will not log you off while there are open documents or 'Do you want to save this file?' program messages to respond to. However, Windows XP comes equipped with what is arguably its best feature of all (we'd argue the point anyway): Fast User Switching. So long as this option is checked in User Accounts (step 4 above), a new user can log on and start a Windows session without the current user logging off first. Open programs remain open, running tasks keep running, and an internet connection stays live during the switch.

In a typical scenario, you might be working at your computer with 17 windows open, six background tasks running and a massive download in progress (it's typical around here, anyway). Along comes another user desperate to check for an important e-mail. Now, normally this would mean saving your files and restarting the computer, not to mention an argument, but with Fast User Switching enabled you can let the other user log on to check e-mail (or do anything else) without in any way affecting your work. Click Start, Log Off and then click Switch User. Alternatively, press the Windows and L keys simultaneously.

The Welcome screen now appears, at which point any user can log on. Just to reiterate: the current Windows session continues in the meantime, out of sight but unaffected by a second user logging on. To return to your session, the second user should log out or use Fast User Switching again. Either option brings back the Welcome screen, at which point you can click your icon and log back on to the interrupted Windows session.

With Fast User Switching enabled, two or more users can have Windows sessions running concurrently.

If you uncheck the Welcome screen option in User Accounts, each user has to type in his name and password at the log on prompt. This also disables Fast User Switching.

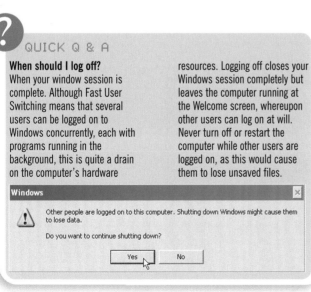

? QUICK Q & A

When should I log off?
When your window session is complete. Although Fast User Switching means that several users can be logged on to Windows concurrently, each with programs running in the background, this is quite a drain on the computer's hardware resources. Logging off closes your Windows session completely but leaves the computer running at the Welcome screen, whereupon other users can log on at will. Never turn off or restart the computer while other users are logged on, as this would cause them to lose unsaved files.

Privacy and passwords

There are some important privacy considerations with Windows XP's User Accounts feature. Each user has his own My Documents folder, but any administrator can open it simply by going to C:\Documents and Settings\User Name. A limited user has no such right of access, which is one very good reason for only granting administrator status to accounts that really need it, but administrators have no secrets from one another by default. This, however, can be changed... a bit.

Keeping folders private

Any limited user or administrator can prevent prying by taking steps to explicitly protect his folders. To do this, first log on. Then:

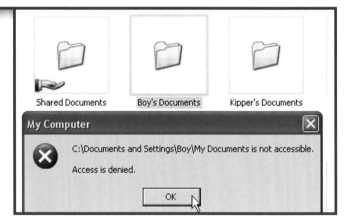

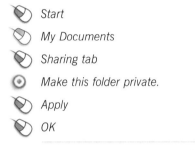

- 🖱 *Start*
- 🖱 *My Documents*
- 🖱 *Sharing tab*
- ◉ *Make this folder private.*
- 🖱 *Apply*
- 🖱 *OK*

Now no other user, even an administrator, can look inside this folder.

To make your entire user profile private in one move, log on, go to C:\Documents and Settings, right-click your user name and follow the same procedure. Be aware that you can only make folders or your user profile private if your hard disk is formatted with NTFS.

One caveat: any administrator can go to User Accounts and change any other user's password without their knowledge. He could then log on as that user and do what he likes. User Accounts are not, therefore, particularly strong on privacy.

Want to see what's in another user's folders? Any administrator can open any other user's My Documents folder from within his own account – unless the folder is made private.

Sharing files with users

Local file sharing – that is, sharing files between different users on the same computer as opposed to across a network – primarily involves the Shared Documents folder: C:\Documents and Settings\All Users\Shared Documents. You will also find shortcuts to Shared Documents in the Tasks View pane in most Explorer windows, including My Documents and My Computer. Whereas every user has his own My Documents folder, there is only one Shared Documents folder and all users, administrator and limited alike, have access to it from their own accounts.

In a nutshell, if you want to share a file or a folder with all other users, copy or move it to Shared Documents.

Windows Explorer provides plenty of shortcuts to the Shared Documents folder. Drag files here to share them with all other users.

Using passwords

A word or two on passwords in User Accounts. The point of a password is obviously to stop anybody but a legitimate user logging on to Windows and using the computer. Passwords are optional in User Accounts, however – see step 3 on p95 – and you might not bother with them on a family PC. But if you do, here are some salient points:

While logged on to his own account, a limited user can change his password. Even if you, an administrator, set up the password in the first place, he can override it to keep you out of his account.

Except that this is pointless because an administrator can change any limited user's password at any time. So, if you found yourself locked out of a limited account, all you would have to do is change the password in User Accounts. Now, of course, the limited user would be locked out of his own account.

But – and this is quite something – any administrator can also change any other administrator's password, or indeed delete his account.

No limited user can change an administrator's password; the option is simply not there in User Accounts. Nor can he access an administrator's files, with the sole exception of files lodged in the Shared Documents folder (see p98).

The bottom line is that password protection only really protects administrators from intrusion by limited users – and the moral is that you should only set up administrator accounts for people you really trust, and who need full control over the computer.

But this is not the end of the story…

The Administrator account revisited

Just to reiterate what we said on p94: all Windows XP computers have a hidden Administrator account that lets you log on with full administrative rights (and more), irrespective of other users and their passwords. All you need to know is a) that an account called Administrator exists; b) that the password is blank; and c) that you can log on as 'the' Administrator only in Safe Mode with XP Home Edition but without restrictions in XP Professional. Armed with this, you can log on to any XP computer regardless of security settings and delete existing User Accounts, change passwords to lock users out, snoop, steal files, or whatever. You could even create a new password for 'the' Administrator account itself to stop anybody else from using it, even in Safe Mode. Five minutes of malevolence is all it takes to render an XP computer completely unusable. Not fun.

It is not possible for somebody to log in as 'the' Administrator remotely – i.e. over a network or across the internet – so the risk is only from people with physical access to your hardware. Does that make you feel more secure?

If not, it follows that you should password-protect the Administrator account, and that you should do it now. This can be done in two ways.

Restart your computer in Safe Mode (press F8 during boot), click the Administrator icon on the Welcome screen to log on, go to User Accounts, select the Administrator account and create a password.

Alternatively,

Start

Run

control userpasswords2

OK

Select Administrator in the User Name column and click the Reset Password button. Now enter a password twice.

As we said, you may never use 'the' Administrator account to start your computer, but at least now you know that you can if you need to, and nobody else can without the password.

In Safe Mode, you can give your Administrator account a secure password.

Reset the default Administrator password from blank to something a little more secure.

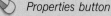
Can I rename 'the' Administrator account to something less obvious?
Yes indeed, and you should consider doing this as well as password-protecting the account.

🖱 Start

🖱 Run

⌨ control userpasswords2

🖱 OK

Highlight the Administrator account in the main window

🖱 Properties button

Now you can rename it to anything you like. Remember that a would-be hacker starts off with two useful bits of knowledge: your computer has a hidden account called Administrator, and the password is blank. By changing both the account name and the password, you keep him doubly in the dark.

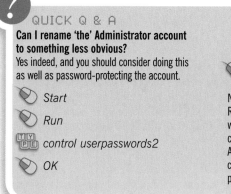

Forgotten password?

Whenever you password-protect a User Account in Windows XP, including 'the' Administrator account, you should take the opportunity to make a Password Reset Disk – just in case.

1

🖱 Start

🖱 Control Panel

🖱 User Accounts

🖱 Open any password-protected account

🖱 Prevent a forgotten password

Pop a blank disk in your floppy drive and run the Forgotten Password Wizard.

2

🖱 Next   🖱 Next

🖱 Next   🖱 Next

⌨ Password   🖱 Finish

Type in your current password when prompted. This rather illustrates the importance of creating the emergency disk now before you've had a chance to forget the password! You now have one emergency password reset disk, which can get you in to this User Account. Make a fresh disk for every password-protected account. But what exactly do you do with them, other than keep them safe?

3

🖱 Use your password reset disk

If and when you mistype a password at the Welcome screen, you should see a prompt that lets you use the reset disk. Simply pop it in the drive and follow the wizard.

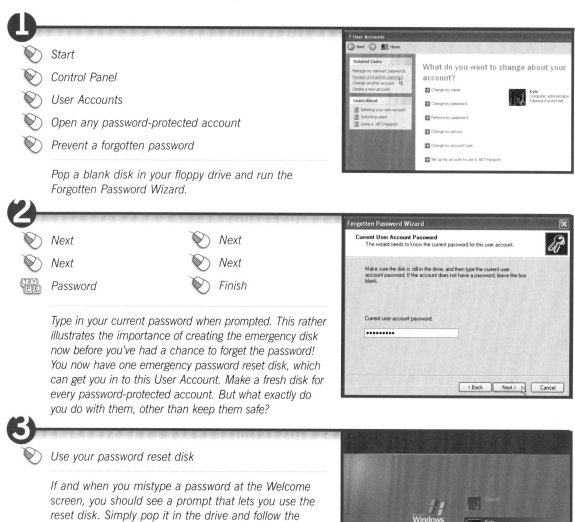

4

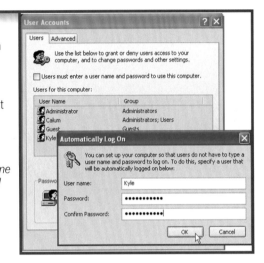

TYPE *New password*

Windows authenticates that the encrypted password on the disk matches the password for this particular User Account (without actually revealing it) and lets you enter a new password. The disk is then modified so that it can be used again should you forget the new password. Finally, the Wizard closes and you can log on to your User Account as normal. Enter the new password at the Welcome screen.

Bypassing passwords

If you appreciate the added security of passwords but frankly can not be bothered to enter one every time you log on to Windows, there is a way to partially circumvent them without sacrificing password protection completely.

Log off any concurrent user sessions and decide which account you wish to nominate as the default.

🖱 *Start*

🖱 *Run*

TYPE *control userpasswords2*

🖱 *OK*

○ *Users must enter a user name and password to use this computer*

🖱 *Apply*

TYPE *your User Account name in the User name field*

TYPE *your password twice*

🖱 *OK*

🖱 *OK*

There's no need to enter a password when you restart your computer if you select a default account here.

This rather elaborate process means that when you restart the computer, Windows will automatically log on the nominated account without halting at the Welcome screen.

Screensaver passwords

When you have User Accounts set up on your computer, a handy new option quietly appears on the screensaver menu

🖱 *Start*

🖱 *Control Panel*

🖱 *Appearance and Themes*

🖱 *Display*

🖱 *Screen Saver tab*

◉ *Select a screensaver and check On resume, display Welcome screen*

Now, when an active screensaver is disturbed, the Welcome screen kicks in rather than a direct return to Windows. This means that users have to enter a password to continue (assuming of course that you password-protect your User Accounts). Additionally, any user can log on from the Welcome screen secure in the knowledge that tasks you have left running or open files left unsaved will be unaffected.

Password protection and quick access to User Accounts combined with the screensaver option.

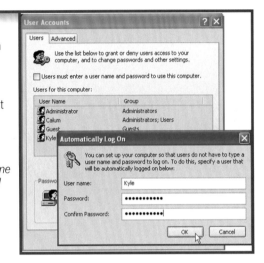

PART 6 Sharing and security

Network sharing

It is, of course, possible to share files and folders in a local network. Windows 2000 users please exhale now: file sharing in Windows XP is child's play.

File Folder

Archive   My Music

A shared folder can be identified in any Explorer window by means of a modified icon. This is less obvious in the List and Details views than in Tiles, Icons or Thumbnails.

A new feature called Simple File Sharing does away with all the 'classic' complexity of selective user-level permissions in favour of a less secure but infinitely more intuitive one-click approach.

You can share selected sub-folders without sharing the parent folder (which is My Documents in this screenshot).

In a nutshell, you can share any file or folder on your computer with all other network users. What you cannot do is share it with some and not others.

A networked user cannot delete or modify a shared file unless you grant change permissions (see Step 2 on p105).

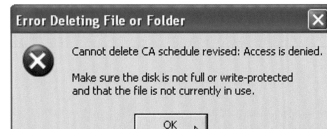

Error Deleting File or Folder

Cannot delete CA schedule revised: Access is denied.

Make sure the disk is not full or write-protected and that the file is not currently in use.

OK

Sharing a folder

In this worked example, we will share a folder on one computer with all other computers on a local network.

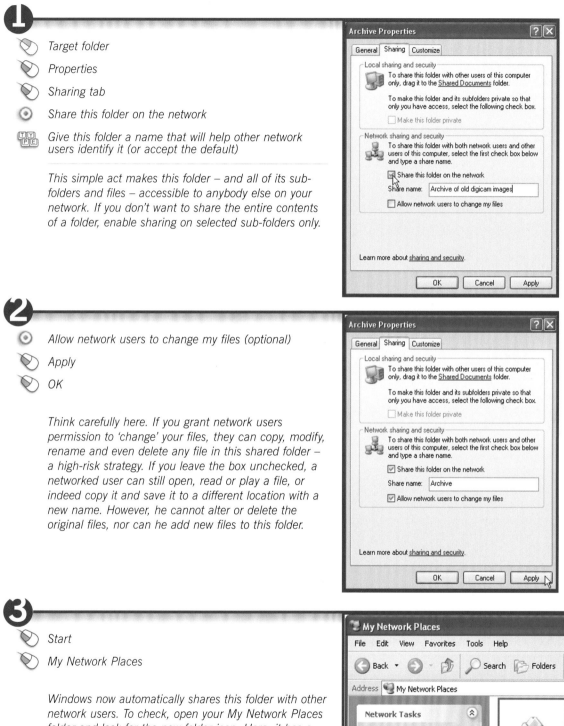

1

🖱️ *Target folder*

🖱️ *Properties*

🖱️ *Sharing tab*

◉ *Share this folder on the network*

⌨️ *Give this folder a name that will help other network users identify it (or accept the default)*

This simple act makes this folder – and all of its sub-folders and files – accessible to anybody else on your network. If you don't want to share the entire contents of a folder, enable sharing on selected sub-folders only.

2

◉ *Allow network users to change my files (optional)*

🖱️ *Apply*

🖱️ *OK*

Think carefully here. If you grant network users permission to 'change' your files, they can copy, modify, rename and even delete any file in this shared folder – a high-risk strategy. If you leave the box unchecked, a networked user can still open, read or play a file, or indeed copy it and save it to a different location with a new name. However, he cannot alter or delete the original files, nor can he add new files to this folder.

3

🖱️ *Start*

🖱️ *My Network Places*

Windows now automatically shares this folder with other network users. To check, open your My Network Places folder and look for the new folder icon. Here, it has a special network-style pipe-like icon; in any other Explorer window, a shared folder is designated by an upward-facing palm symbol. To unshare a folder, repeat steps 1 and 2 and uncheck the boxes.

Using the Shared Documents folder

For an even simpler system than Simple File Sharing, use the Shared Documents folder. When a computer joins a network, its Shared Documents folder is automatically shared i.e. files lodged here are immediately accessible to the entire network. Stick with this and you might not need to manually share any other folders.

Contrariwise, you can unshare Shared Documents on a network without affecting local file sharing i.e. User Account holders on the same machine can still access it.

- Shared Documents (you'll find it in the C:\Documents and Settings\All Users folder)
- Properties
- Sharing tab
- Share this folder on the network
- Apply

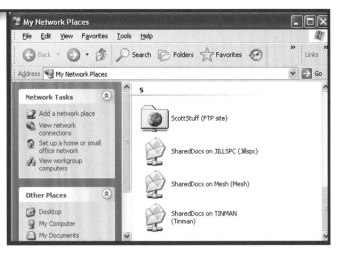

All Shared Documents folders are publicly shared on a network as well as between User Accounts.

XP Professional differences

Whereas Windows XP Home Edition works exclusively with the Simple File Sharing system, Professional owners have the option to revert to Windows 2000-style file sharing. This offers a great deal more flexibility, as share and change permissions are granted on a file-by-file, user-by-user basis. This may appeal or even prove essential in a sensitive commercial environment. Note that your hard disk must be formatted with NTFS.

To disable Simple File Sharing,

- Start
- Control Panel
- Appearance and Themes
- Folder Options
- View tab
- Advanced Settings
- Use Simple File Sharing

At which point, sorry, but you're on your own: this manual is too short for the intricacies of NTFS file permissions.

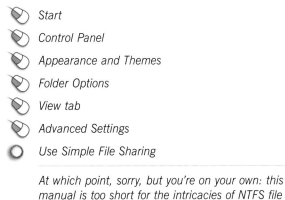

Windows XP Pro users can disable Simple File Sharing in favour of detailed rights and permissions.

My Network Places

Echoing the Shared Documents folder's role in User Accounts is My Network Places, home of network shares. Again, there are ubiquitous links to it in Explorer and it even merits a spot on the Start menu. Whenever a network user shares a folder, a shortcut to it should appear here. In fact, My Network Places is one of four key folders in Windows XP. Just to summarise:

- **My Computer** Explorer's access point to drives and hardware devices
- **My Documents** Private files and folders, integral to your user profile
- **Shared Documents** Public files and folders that anybody with an administrator, limited or Guest User Account can access
- **My Network Places** Files, folders and resources on a network, be it local, wide (e.g. a company network) or the internet

As is the XP style, My Network Places comes with its very own Tasks View pane (called, unsurprisingly, Network Tasks). The tools provided are:

- **Add a network place** This lets you create a shortcut to any locally networked folder or to any location on a wider network, including web and FTP sites (an online file storage service, for instance). We will work with this wizard shortly.
- **View network connections** Here you can edit existing local network and internet connections. The Tasks View pane changes in this window to offer shortcuts to the New Connection Wizard and the Network Setup Wizard (as seen on p80 and p84 respectively).
- **Set up a home or small office network** This is just the Network Setup Wizard again.
- **View workgroup computers** This opens the top-level workgroup folder, usually called Mshome (or MSHOME) unless you changed the workgroup name during setup (Step 6 on p87). Here you can see at a glance which networked computers are currently connected.

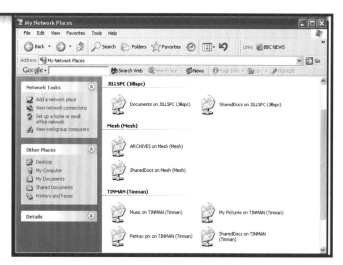

My Network Places provides shortcuts to all networked folders.

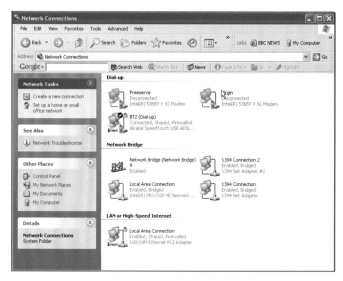

Internet and local network connections displayed as icons.

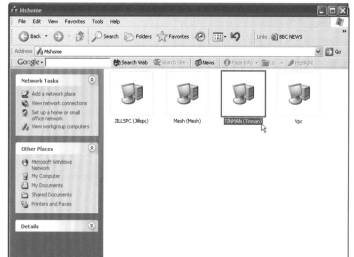

Here we see four networked computers. Should one go offline – i.e. disconnect from the network – its icon would disappear.

Adding a Network Place

In our experience, My Network Places does not always work exactly as expected. If you find that a Shared Documents folder or any manually shared folder fails to show up here, conduct a network search and add a shortcut yourself.

1

- *Start*
- *My Network Places*
- *Add a network place*

A network place can be a shared folder on your local network or any location on a wider network, including an internet site. For now, we are concerned with a local network.

2

- *Next*
- *Next*

The Add Network Place Wizard launches and attempts to download information about service providers. Ignore all this. Wait for the invitation to choose another network location.

3

- *Browse*
- *Entire Network*
- *Microsoft Windows Network*
- *Mshome (or the name of your local network)*

- *Name of user's PC*
- *SharedDocs (or whichever shared folder you are looking for)*
- *OK*

This is a case of navigating shared resources on networked computers. Here, we hone in on the Shared Documents folder (which always shows up as SharedDocs on a network) located on a workgroup computer called Jillspc. If you cannot find a shared folder with this method, it has not been correctly configured for network sharing (see p105).

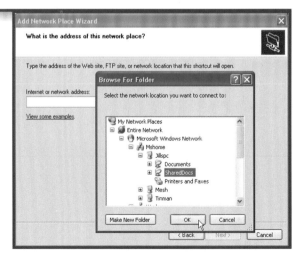

4

🖱 *Next*

⌨ *Give the folder a name*

🖱 *Next*

The first screen confirms the network path to the shared folder. In the next screen, you have the opportunity to name the folder. This only affects how the folder is displayed in your own My Network Places folder – i.e. it does not actually rename the folder – so feel free to modify it.

5

🖱 *Finish*

The Wizard confirms the results of your action and concludes. The new shortcut should appear immediately in your My Network Places folder; if not, right-click inside the window and click Refresh from the popup menu. You can access this shared folder directly from My Network Places at any time, providing the host computer is running and connected to the network.

?

QUICK Q & A

Should I share my entire C: drive in a family network where privacy is not a problem?
Best not to. The trouble is that another user might inadvertently muck up your system settings, up to and including breaking

Windows. Move or copy the files and folders you wish to share to the Shared Documents folder and/or work your way through your folders in Explorer and enable selective network sharing on a folder-by-folder basis.

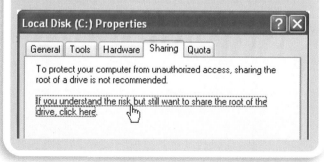

?

QUICK Q & A

Is there any easy way to see which folders I currently have shared on my local network?
Aside from the My Network Places folder, try this. Click Start > Control Panel > Performance

and Maintenance > Administrative Tools > Computer Management, and expand the Shared Folders entry. All your network shares appear in the main window to the right.

PART ⑥ Sharing printers

With printer sharing enabled in a network, any computer can send documents to any printer regardless of which computer it is physically attached to – or, in the case of a printer with an Ethernet port, even if it is not connected to any computer at all but rather plugs straight in to a network hub or switch.

Sharing a printer

Here, we will share a printer that is installed on one networked computer and then connect to it from another.

Networked printers can be accessed from any program's Print menu.

1

🖱 *Start*

🖱 *Printers and Other Hardware*

🖱 *View installed printers or fax machines*

This opens the Printers and Faxes folder.

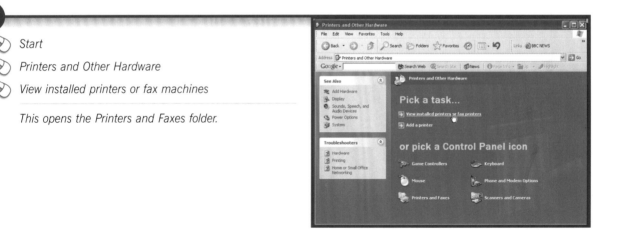

2

🖱 *Printer icon*

🖱 *Sharing...*

Locate the printer in question – a Canon device in this case – and select Sharing from the popup menu.

3

🖱 *Sharing tab*

⊙ *Share this printer*

⌨ *Printer name*

🖱 *Apply*

🖱 *OK*

Enable sharing and give the printer a friendly name that will help you and others identify it on the network.

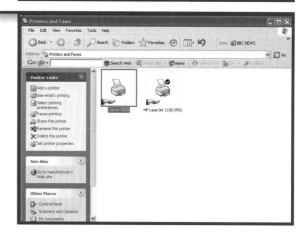

4

Back in the Printers and Faxes folder (repeat Step 1), confirm that the printer icon now has the upturned-palm symbol that signifies a local device configured for network sharing.

5

🖱 *Add a printer*

🖱 *Next*

To make this printer accessible to other computers on the network, open the Printers and Faxes folder on each in turn (Step 1 again). But this time, launch the Add Printer Wizard.

6

⊙ *A network printer, or a printer attached to another computer*

🖱 *Next*

Making the correct choice here is vital as you need the wizard to search for printers that are not physically connected to this computer.

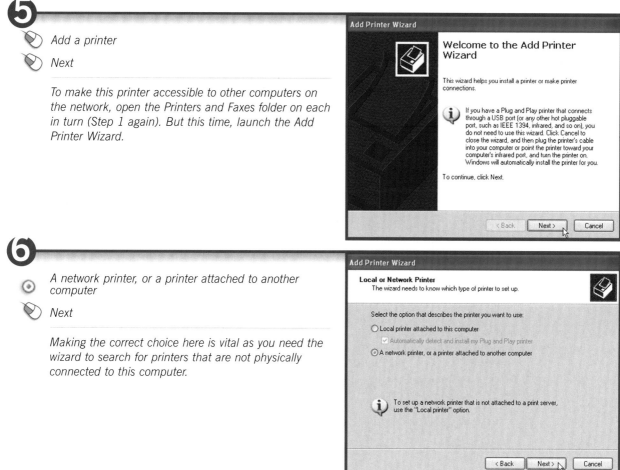

7

○ *Browse for a printer*

🖱 *Next*

You could manually input the address of the printer but it's easier to let the wizard detect all available networked printers.

8

🖱 *Printer*

🖱 *Next*

This is the only slightly tricky bit. The wizard displays a list of networked computers along with any shared printers, but unfortunately it refers to each computer's workgroup name rather than its more helpful descriptive name (see Step 5 on p86). Look for the printer name that you stipulated in Step 3, and select it.

9

🖱 *Yes*

🖱 *Finish*

The wizard fires off a warning about the risks inherent in installing printer drivers. Click Yes to bypass such paranoia and allow the wizard to complete.

10

An icon for the newly-shared network printer duly appears in the printer's folder, complete with the network pipe symbol. If this is the only printer available to this computer, it automatically becomes the default printer; if not, you can make it so with a right-click. From now on, you can send documents to this printer from any program just as easily as if it was attached to this computer.

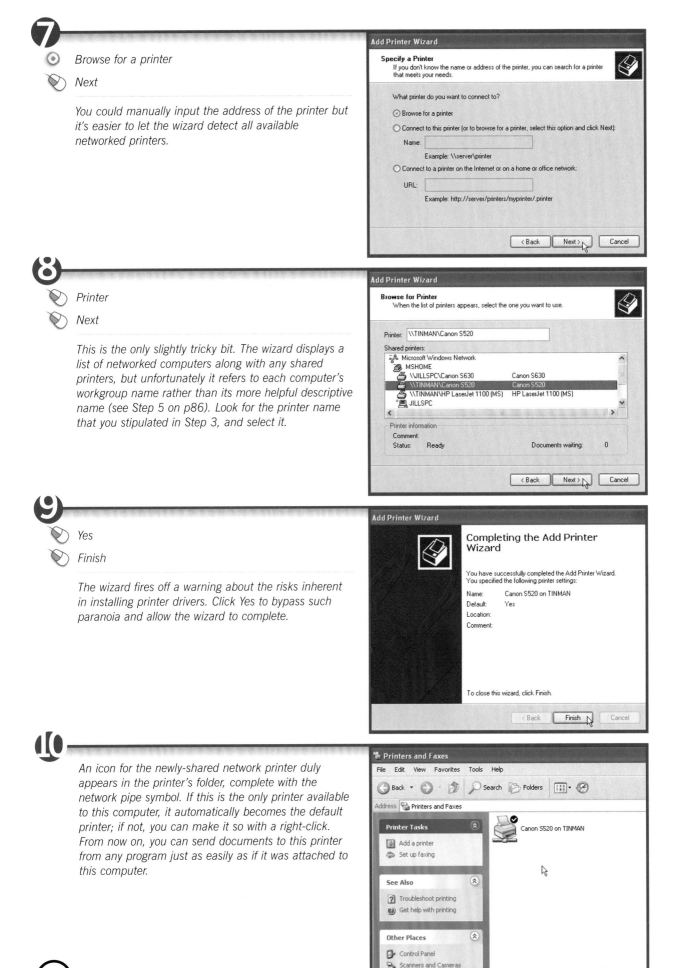

Printer icons

You can get to the Printer and Faxes folders from My Network Places as well as via the Control Panel. Look in the Other Places section of the Tasks View pane. Here, along with shortcuts to all the usual suspects – the Desktop, My Computer, My Documents and Shared Documents – is a link to networked Printers and Faxes.

Printer icons reveal the status of the device. An upturned palm denotes a shared local printer; a pipe-like icon denotes a remote networked device; and a transparent icon tells you that the printer is currently offline (i.e. turned off or otherwise disconnected from the network).

In this screenshot, we see one offline, local, shared printer (Canon S520); one online, remote, networked printer (Canon S630 on Jill); and one online, local, shared printer (HP Laserjet 1100). The tick on the Laserjet icon further tells us that this is the default printer for this computer.

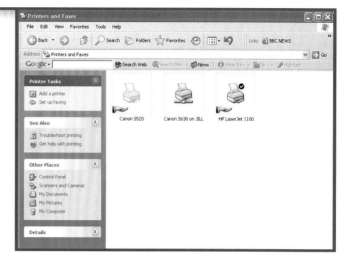

A printer icon shows you its status.

Printer drivers

In Step 3 above, there is an option to install additional drivers. This is useful if one or more computers on your network is running an older version of Windows, as Windows XP will store a copy of the appropriate driver in readiness for a sharing request. You will need the printer's installation CD-ROM here; just pop it in the drive when prompted. If all networked computers are running XP, the Add Printer wizard takes care of everything and sharing is seamless.

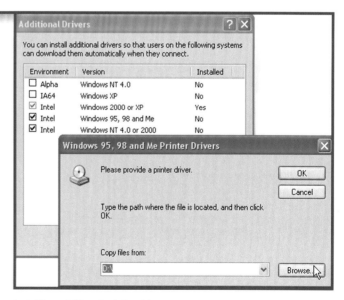

Installing additional printer drivers lets non-XP computers share access to a networked printer.

PART **6** Sharing drives

You can easily share a CD or DVD drive in a network. One benefit is being able to install programs on networked computers directly from the shared drive rather than taking the CD-ROM from one to the other. Another, probably more useful, purpose is sharing access to an application that pulls content from a DVD disc (such as a multimedia encyclopaedia) rather than installing completely to the hard drive; so long as the program files are installed locally, the DVD itself can be left in a shared DVD drive and networked computers can call upon it as and when required. You can even stream DVD movies from a shared drive to a networked computer so long as the remote computer has a software DVD player program.

1

Start

My Computer

Drive to be shared

Sharing and Security

Sharing tab

If you understand the risk…

Windows forces you to override a protective warning here. The problem with sharing the root of a drive is that anybody with access to it has complete control. This, however, is only a concern with hard drives (see Quick Q & A on p109). Confirm that you wish to proceed.

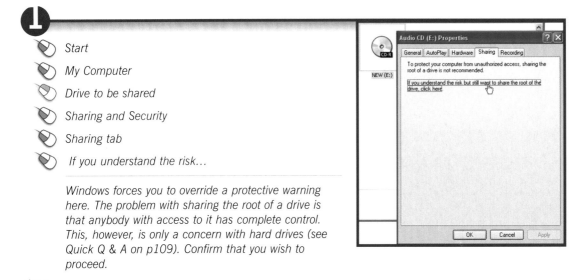

2

Share this folder on the Network

Name

Apply

OK

Give the drive a recognisable name. Leave the Allow network users to change my files box unchecked. Now anybody on your network can read, play and copy the contents of any disc in this drive.

Mapping network drives

Although a shared drive appears as just another folder in My Network Places, you may need to run the Add Network Place wizard first, as described on p108. It can also be beneficial to 'map' the drive on a networked computer, particularly if locally-installed programs will call upon it. So far as Windows and other programs are concerned, this makes a shared drive behave just like a 'real', local drive.

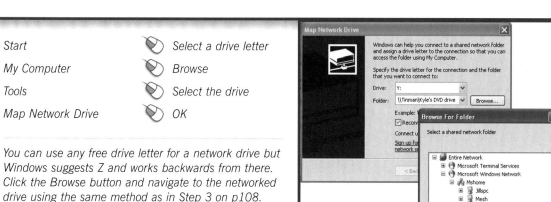

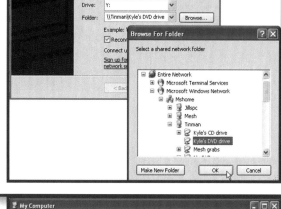

- Start
- My Computer
- Tools
- Map Network Drive
- Select a drive letter
- Browse
- Select the drive
- OK

You can use any free drive letter for a network drive but Windows suggests Z and works backwards from there. Click the Browse button and navigate to the networked drive using the same method as in Step 3 on p108. Look for the name you assigned in Step 2 above.

Back in My Computer, a networked drive is now directly accessible just as if it was attached to the local computer. In this screenshot – Tiles view with icons arranged by type and shown in groups – a networked DVD drive appears as Y: drive and a networked CD drive as Z: drive.

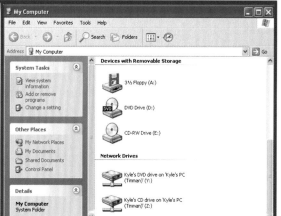

QUICK Q & A

Can I burn my own CDs with Windows XP?
Yes, providing you have a CD writer drive (CD-R or CD-RW). It is not a terribly flexible or fast process, however, and we recommend using a third-party utility like Nero Burning ROM (www.nero.com) or Easy CD Creator (www.roxio.com) for anything more involved than a simple data backup. To use XP's built-in burning capabilities, simply pop a writeable CD in the drive and copy, move or send target files straight to it.

115

File encryption

Windows XP Professional includes a file encryption system called, remarkably enough, Encrypting File System (EFS). Your hard disk must be formatted with NTFS for this to work and unfortunately EFS is not included at all with XP Home Edition, presumably on the premise that only 'professionals' have sensitive information in need of protection. Be that as it may, there are some good third-party encryption utilities around that do not require NTFS, or indeed Windows XP, so in our opinion EFS is not by itself sufficient reason to pay the premium for Professional.

Encrypting a folder

Encryption is essentially a matter of scrambling data to make it unreadable. This data can be unscrambled, or decrypted, on demand but only by someone with access to the original encryption 'key'. EFS uses a system whereby encryption keys are unlocked with a personal 'certificate' that is in turn tied to your User Account. It's all rather complicated behind the scenes but in practice it means that files encrypted by you can only be decrypted by you, and then only when you are logged on to your computer with your personal User Account.

It is in fact surprisingly easy to use EFS. First, log on as normal. If you do not have User Accounts set up on your computer, the default Owner administrator account is fine (see p92).

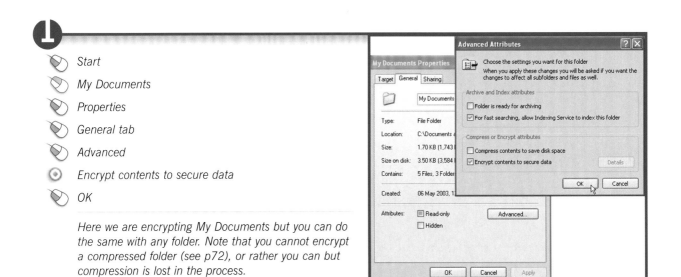

Start

My Documents

Properties

General tab

Advanced

Encrypt contents to secure data

OK

Here we are encrypting My Documents but you can do the same with any folder. Note that you cannot encrypt a compressed folder (see p72), or rather you can but compression is lost in the process.

2

 Apply

⊙ *Apply changes to this folder, subfolders and files*

 OK

This ensures that all existing files within My Documents are encrypted. Any files subsequently moved or copied to this folder, or saved within it, are also automatically encrypted on the fly.

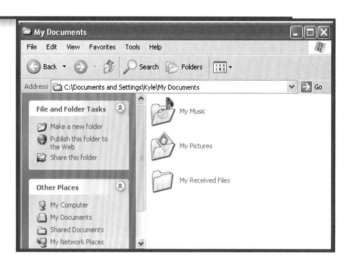

3

 My Documents

Encrypted files and folders are differentiated with a green font in Windows Explorer. You can now work with these files exactly as usual, but only when logged on with your User Account. No other user, even an Administrator, can access your encrypted files (although a malevolent or careless Administrator could move, rename or even delete them).

Copy your EFS certificate

EFS hinges upon certificates that are intrinsically entwined with User Accounts. Should your user profile become corrupted or your User Account deleted, you would be unable to reopen your encrypted files – ever. Therefore it is important to back up your certificate. This can be reinstalled at any time. Note that a certificate is only created when you encrypt your first folder so do not try the following procedure until then.

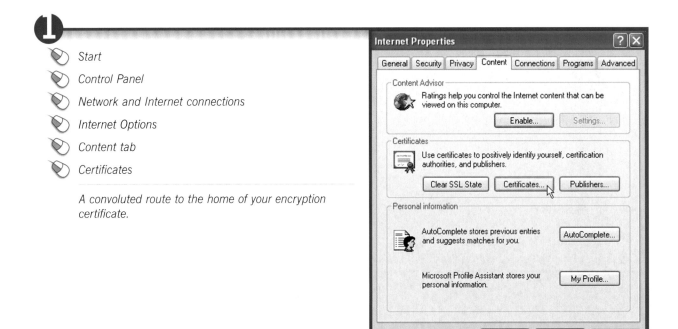

1

Start

Control Panel

Network and Internet connections

Internet Options

Content tab

Certificates

A convoluted route to the home of your encryption certificate.

2

Your certificate

Export

Next

Your encryption certificate appears here. Highlight it and click Export.

3

○ Yes, export the private key

🖱 Next

Confirm that you wish to export a copy of the certificate. This in no way affects the original or impacts upon folders that you have already encrypted.

Certificate Export Wizard

Export Private Key
You can choose to export the private key with the certificate.

Private keys are password protected. If you want to export the private key with the certificate, you must type a password on a later page.

Do you want to export the private key with the certificate?

● Yes, export the private key

○ No, do not export the private key

< Back   Next >   Cancel

4

🖱 Next

Leave the default options as they are and click Next.

Certificate Export Wizard

Export File Format
Certificates can be exported in a variety of file formats.

Select the format you want to use:

○ DER encoded binary X.509 (.CER)

○ Base-64 encoded X.509 (.CER)

○ Cryptographic Message Syntax Standard - PKCS #7 Certificates (.P7B)

☐ Include all certificates in the certification path if possible

● Personal Information Exchange - PKCS #12 (.PFX)

☐ Include all certificates in the certification path if possible

☑ Enable strong protection (requires IE 5.0, NT 4.0 SP4 or above)

☐ Delete the private key if the export is successful

< Back   Next >   Cancel

5

⌨ Password

⌨ Password

Enter and confirm a password. Make it a good one.

Certificate Export Wizard

Password
To maintain security, you must protect the private key by using a password.

Type and confirm a password.

Password:
****

Confirm password:
****

< Back   Next >   Cancel

6

🖱 Browse

⌨ File name

🖱 Next

🖱 Finish

Use the Browse button to select a destination for your exported certificate and give it a file name. The wizard now saves a password-protected copy of your encryption key as a file with a .PFX extension. Save this file to some form of removable media and keep it safe.

Certificate Export Wizard

File to Export
Specify the name of the file you want to export

File name:
C:\Documents and Settings\Kyle\Desktop\mycert.pfx   Browse...

< Back   Next >   Cancel

Reinstalling an EFS certificate

You would reinstall your EFS certificate if:

- Your User Account profile is lost or corrupted.
- You want to work with encrypted files on another Windows XP Professional computer, in which case you must take your certificate with you.
- You want to allow another local user to access your encrypted files, in which case he needs to install a copy of your certificate in his own User Account.

Here we will install a saved EFS certificate on a different computer. First, log on with the User Account that you wish to enable with your certificate. Follow steps 1 and 2 above to open the Certificates window.

1

Import

Certificate file

Open

Next

Ensure that Personal Information Exchange appears in the Files of type field and navigate to your saved .PFX file.

2

Password

Next

Enter the password you assigned when you first exported the file (Step 5 on p.119). Leave the two options unchecked.

3

Place all certificates in the following store

Next

Finish

The Certificate store field should say Personal. If not, use the Browse button to select Personal from the list of possible 'stores'. Click Next and then Finish to complete the import. Now anybody who logs on with this User Account can access files encrypted with this certificate. To delete a certificate, use the Remove button in Step 2 on p118.

Some points to note

Encryption may be transparent and seamless but there are a few important considerations:

- Encryption is essentially uncrackable. This is why backing up your EFS certificate is vital; without it, encrypted files will remain forever inaccessible
- Encryption does not hide the existence of files or disguise file names.
- You can encrypt individual files as well as folders in just the same way.
- If you copy or move an encrypted file or folder to a computer running XP Professional where the hard disk is formatted with NTFS, it stays encrypted. However, if you move or copy it to a FAT-formatted disk or to a Windows XP Home Edition computer, it becomes decrypted.
- If you copy an encrypted file to a floppy disk or writeable CD, encryption is lost (because such media does not support NTFS). To retain encryption, wrap up your files in a Windows Backup Utility archive.

Start

All Programs

Accessories

System Tools

The resulting archive can then be copied to removable media without loss of encryption.

To summarise, you can work with encrypted files on any Windows XP Professional computer so long as it uses NTFS and you import a copy of the certificate with which the files were originally encrypted.

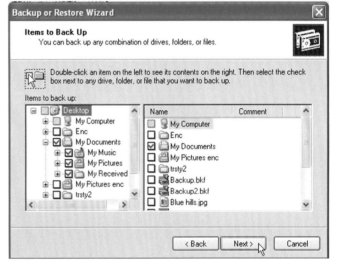

Use Backup when you copy encrypted files to removable media to preserve encryption.

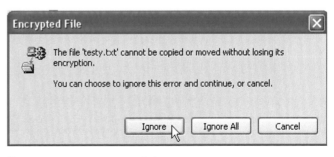

If you move or copy an encrypted file to a FAT disk, encryption is sacrificed.

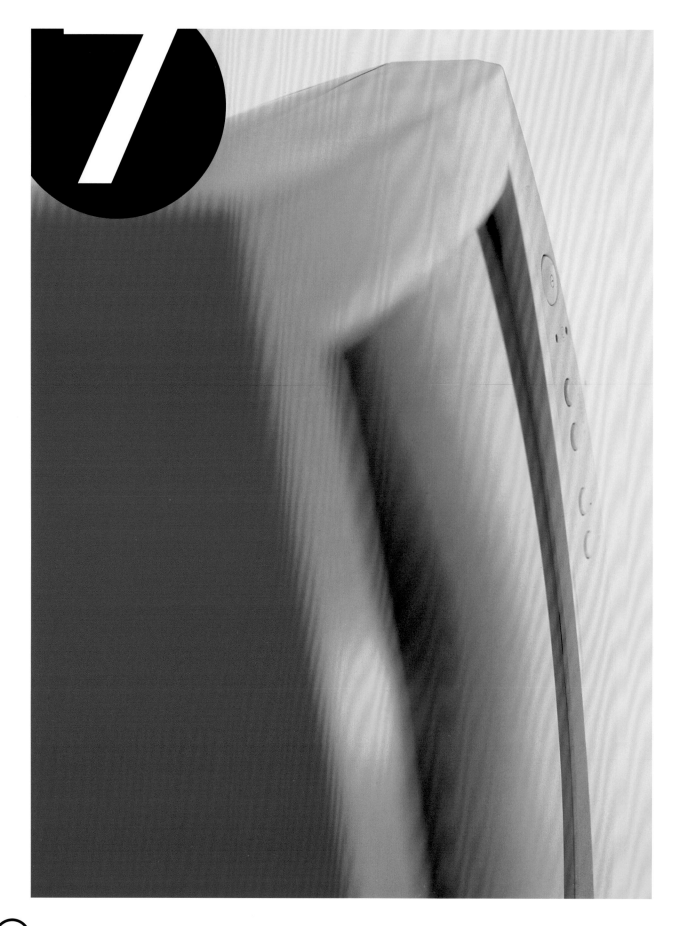

7

PART 7

Instant messaging and more

Windows Messenger

Windows Messenger is an 'instant messaging' program used to communicate with other people across the internet, primarily through text-based 'chat' but also by voice and even with live video. Additionally, you can exchange files, collaborate simultaneously on documents and share a 'whiteboard'.

All grown up now?

Thanks in part to the preponderance of 'emoticons' or 'smileys' (silly symbols that express your mood when words alone are insufficient) and its heritage in internet chat rooms, instant messaging is often thought of more as a toy than a serious communications tool. But this is unfair. In an age of always-on broadband connections, instant messaging is a must-have application. In some circumstances, it is even a powerful alternative to e-mail: rather than e-mailing a friend or colleague and waiting for a response (all the while wondering whether they received your message in the first place), an instant messenger program informs you the moment they come online and lets you strike up a discourse.

Windows Messenger is of course only one of many instant messaging services freely available to anybody with an internet connection. Others include ICQ (for geeks), Yahoo! Messenger (for anybody) and AOL Instant Messenger (the best of the bunch, in our view). There is also a similar Microsoft program called MSN Messenger. However, Windows Messenger deserves special consideration here because it is built right in to Windows XP and integrates very nicely with a couple of innovative and genuinely useful features, as we shall see.

Instant messaging is like e-mail without the delay. Smileys are optional.

PART 1

WINDOWS XP

.NET Passport account

Although Windows Messenger is included with Windows XP, before you can use it you must sign up for a .NET Passport. This gives you access to an internet directory and server which stores details of your contacts – i.e. other Windows Messenger users with whom you communicate – and passes messages from one contact to another.

A password-protected .NET Passport securely identifies you as you and not an impostor, the idea being that you can use your Passport to access a Hotmail e-mail account, make online purchases (providing you pre-register your credit card details) and more. It is also tied to your User Account, with the result that Passport-enabled features remain available so long as you stay logged on.

Microsoft's .NET initiative has yet to change the face of the internet in general or e-commerce in particular – see www.microsoft.com/net for the big picture – and you need to consider carefully whether you sign up for a scheme that may have potential repercussions beyond instant messaging alone. But that's the way it is: Windows Messenger requires an active Passport.

.NET: 'a set of Microsoft software technologies that help connect information, people, systems, and devices through the use of Web services', apparently.

Signing up for a Passport

To get a .NET Passport, you can either register a free Hotmail account (www.hotmail.com) or use a Windows XP wizard. We will take the latter path here. Note that the signup procedure may vary slightly from the one outlined here.

First, open an internet connection so that your computer is online.

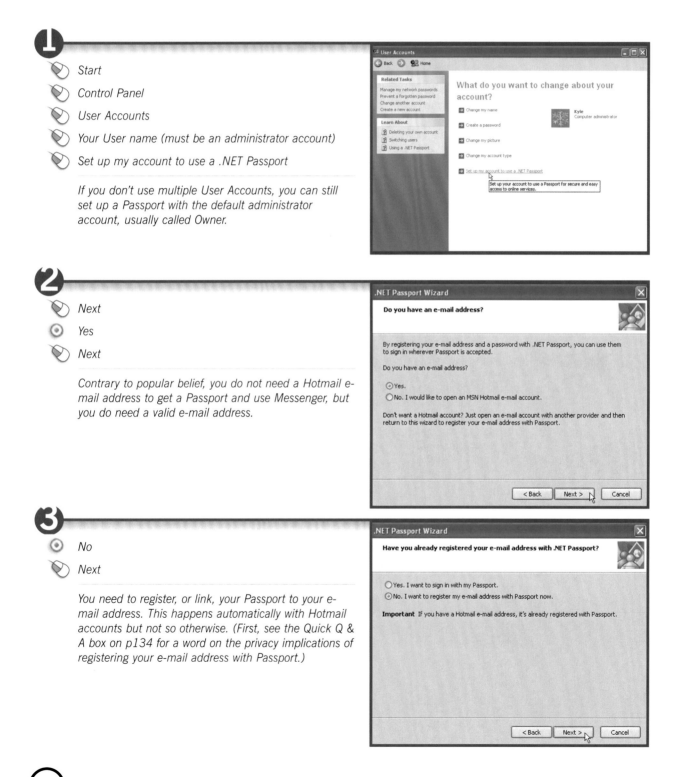

1

Start

Control Panel

User Accounts

Your User name (must be an administrator account)

Set up my account to use a .NET Passport

If you don't use multiple User Accounts, you can still set up a Passport with the default administrator account, usually called Owner.

2

Next

Yes

Next

Contrary to popular belief, you do not need a Hotmail e-mail address to get a Passport and use Messenger, but you do need a valid e-mail address.

3

No

Next

You need to register, or link, your Passport to your e-mail address. This happens automatically with Hotmail accounts but not so otherwise. (First, see the Quick Q & A box on p134 for a word on the privacy implications of registering your e-mail address with Passport.)

4

Next

Next

Complete form

I Agree

Continue

The wizard now launches your default web browser – probably Internet Explorer – and asks you to complete a one-page registration form. Eventually, the browser closes and you return to the Passport wizard.

Microsoft® .NET Passport
Member Services
Registration

Completing this form will register you with .NET Passport Web Site and with Microsoft® .NET Passport. With .NET Passport, you can use the e-mail address and password you provide below to sign in to any site that has the .NET Passport sign-in button.

Sign In

Click the .NET Passport sign-in button if you have already registered for a .NET Passport at another site. (All @hotmail.com and @msn.com e-mail addresses are .NET Passports.)

Fields marked with ☑ will be stored in your .NET Passport.   Help

E-mail Address   kyle

Password
                        Six-character minimum; no spaces

Retype Password

Secret Question   Favorite pet's name?

5

○ Associate my Passport with my Windows User Account

Next

Hmm. If you associate Passport with your User Account, you will be automatically signed in to websites and services that support the Passport protocol simply by virtue of being logged on to Windows. We have yet to find this necessary or even appealing, so here we choose to leave the option unchecked.

.NET Passport Wizard

Associate your .NET Passport with your Windows user account?

Windows can help make Passport sign-in at participating sites easy by associating your Passport with your Windows user account. To associate your Passport with your user account, click **Next**.

If you don't want to associate your Passport with your user account, clear the check box before you click **Next**.

☐ Associate my Passport with my Windows user account.

< Back   Next >   Cancel

6

Finish

The wizard completes and your Passport account is ready to use. Close the User Accounts window and return to the Desktop.

.NET Passport Wizard

You're done!

Your Windows XP user account is now set up to use the following .NET Passport:

kyle.macrae@btinternet.com

To close this wizard, click Finish.

< Back   Finish   Cancel

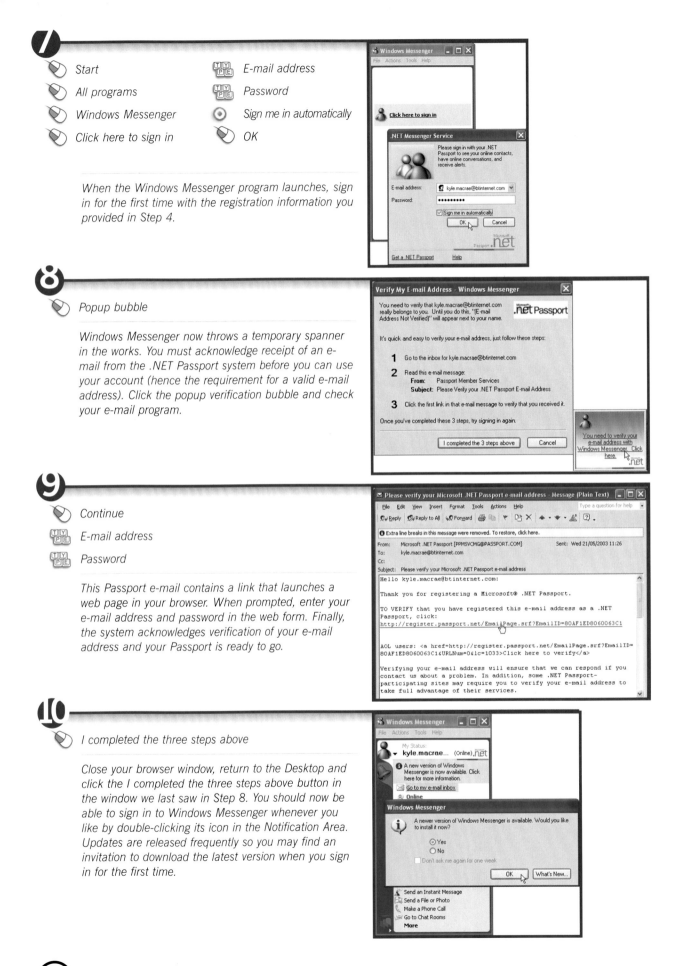

7

- Start
- All programs
- Windows Messenger
- Click here to sign in
- E-mail address
- Password
- Sign me in automatically
- OK

When the Windows Messenger program launches, sign in for the first time with the registration information you provided in Step 4.

8

- Popup bubble

Windows Messenger now throws a temporary spanner in the works. You must acknowledge receipt of an e-mail from the .NET Passport system before you can use your account (hence the requirement for a valid e-mail address). Click the popup verification bubble and check your e-mail program.

9

- Continue
- E-mail address
- Password

This Passport e-mail contains a link that launches a web page in your browser. When prompted, enter your e-mail address and password in the web form. Finally, the system acknowledges verification of your e-mail address and your Passport is ready to go.

10

- I completed the three steps above

Close your browser window, return to the Desktop and click the I completed the three steps above button in the window we last saw in Step 8. You should now be able to sign in to Windows Messenger whenever you like by double-clicking its icon in the Notification Area. Updates are released frequently so you may find an invitation to download the latest version when you sign in for the first time.

Managing contacts

Contacts are the very essence of Windows Messenger – or any other instant messenger service, for that matter. In this context, a contact is another Messenger user with whom you chat, exchange files, share applications, videoconference or whatever. By default, Windows Messenger starts with Windows and runs constantly in the background, visible only as an icon in the Notification Area. Double-click this icon to open the main program window. Contacts who are currently online are listed in the top part of the upper section and offline contacts below them. This is the beauty and simplicity of instant messaging and, in fact, the aspect of it that never fails to take newcomers by surprise. How does it work?

Online or offline?

If you allow Windows Messenger to run in the background, it connects to the .NET service the moment you connect to the internet. You now have an open link to the messaging servers. The .NET service then looks for all instances of Windows Messenger programs in which you are listed as a contact and alerts them that your status has changed. That is, anybody who has you in their contact list sees your name shift from the offline to the online section and knows that you are, in principle at least, available for a chat. This status-monitoring is transparent and very nearly instantaneous, and enables you to keep tabs on all your contacts.

A little clarification here. Normally, 'online' means 'connected to the internet'. In the context of instant messaging, however, online means a) connected to the internet and b) signed into .NET with your Passport and c) running the Windows Messenger program. Windows XP does its hardest to equate these two definitions but you may find it all rather intrusive. After all, perhaps you just want to check e-mail or surf for a while without the world and his wife knowing that you are sitting at your computer or interrupting. If so, you should take steps to tame Windows Messenger. We discuss this on p133.

Adding a contact

Before you can use Windows Messenger for instant messaging, you must add a contact or two to your contact list. Here's how.

(You)

  Add a Contact

  By e-mail address or sign-in name option

  Next

  Contact's e-mail address

This requires that you know which e-mail address your contact registered with .NET Passport (the best bet is to ask them). The Search option only works if your contact chose to be listed in the Hotmail directory (unlikely).

② (You)

Finish

If the e-mail address is recognised (i.e. registered with Passport), your contact is added to your Windows Messenger window and you can see immediately whether they are on- or offline.

③ (Your contact)

⊙ *Allow this person to see when you are online and contact you*

⊙ *Add this person to my contact list*

🖱 *OK*

Simultaneously, your contact receives a popup alert to the effect that you have added him to your contact list. This is an important privacy feature, and one you will see yourself when somebody adds you to their contact list. If you do not recognise a contact's name or e-mail address, or simply do not want him as a contact, check the Block option.

④ (You)

🖱 *Contact name*

 *Anything at all...*

To initiate a chat, double-click a contact's name and start typing in lower part of the chat window. Your contact is alerted to the fact that you want to talk and can respond or ignore you as they choose. Just to state the obvious: it is only possible to have an instant messaging session when both parties are online, both are signed into their Passport accounts, and both have the Windows Messenger program running.

Things you can do with Windows Messenger

Windows Messenger is ever-evolving and who knows what communications tools it will provide in the future? For now, here are just a few of our favourite features.

Change your contact name

By default, Windows Messenger displays your e-mail address in other people's contact lists. You might prefer to be known by your first name, full name or a nickname. With Windows Messenger running,

 Tools

 Options

 Personal tab

> *Enter whatever you like in the My .Net Service Display Name field. The change is immediate. This is how you will appear to your contacts from now on.*

A friendly buddy name is a more attractive option than being identified by your e-mail address.

Send and receive e-mail

Well, up to a point. If you registered a Hotmail address with your Passport account (Step 3 on p126), Windows Messenger monitors it on your behalf and alerts you when new messages arrive. This does not work with other e-mail services. To send an e-mail,

 a contact

 Send E-mail.

> *This either launches your default e-mail program (Outlook Express, Outlook or whatever) or takes you to your Hotmail account, depending.*

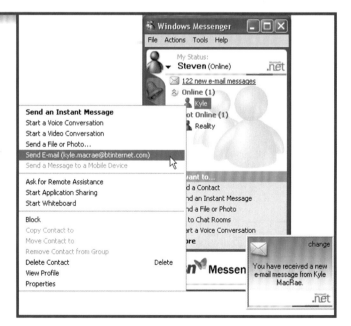

Windows Messenger integrates with e-mail, particularly if you use Hotmail.

Exchange files

Very useful indeed, this one, particularly if your ISP imposes daft – sorry, sensible bandwidth-conserving – restrictions on the size of e-mail attachments. One contact can send another a file of any size through the internet with Windows Messenger.

Highlight the appropriate contact in your list and click Send a File or Photo. Now browse to the file on your hard disk (or other drive) and click Open. Your contact may accept or refuse the file, whereupon the transfer either starts or fails. It is not possible to impose a file transfer upon a reluctant recipient, nor can anybody send you a file without your express say-so. The speed of file transfers depends mainly upon the speed of each contact's internet connection. It should go without saying that you should scan a received file for viruses before launching or viewing it.

Windows Messenger automatically creates a new folder in your My Documents folder called My Received Files in which incoming file transfers are saved by default. You can change this if you like by

Tools

Options

Preferences

and specifying a different folder in the File Transfers field.

File transfers are permission-based, so only accept a file if you know and trust the contact and you actually want the file.

Talk to your contacts

With the requisite hardware – a sound card, a microphone and speakers or headphones – you can use Windows Messenger to talk to and hear your contacts. Messenger connects you directly to known contacts through the .NET service so there is no fussing with IP addresses and fancy configurations. In short, it works and it's free.

Tools

Audio Tuning Wizard

to set up your hardware, and then initiate a call with the Start a Voice Conversation link in the lower section of the main Windows Messenger window. As always, requests like this are permission-based so a contact can decline to take part.

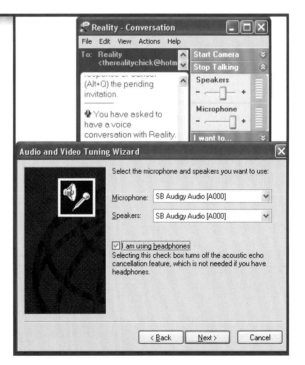

Use the Audio Tuning Wizard to configure your microphone and speakers/headphones for voice chat.

See and be seen

In a natural extension of voice chat, you can use a webcam – or any other video device, like a camcorder – to transmit live video images as you communicate. Any contact can receive a video stream whether or not they have their own webcam, although two-way videoconferencing is obviously more fun. As always, a broadband connection helps.

So long as your webcam or device is correctly configured to work with Windows XP, Windows Messenger takes care of the details. Plug it in, initiate a text or voice chat with a contact, and click Start Camera.

Face-to-face chat is easy with Windows Messenger – all you need is a webcam.

Turn it off

Not everybody likes or needs instant messaging, and not everybody appreciates having Windows Messenger start automatically with Windows. To stop this behaviour,

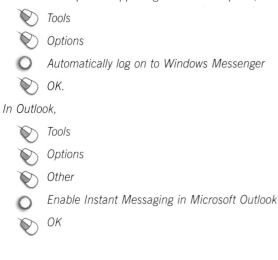

Tools

Options

Preferences

Run this program when Windows starts.

Normally, when you 'close' the program window in the normal way by clicking the cross in the top right-hand corner of the window, Messenger merely shrinks to a Notification Area icon and continues to run in the background, monitoring incoming e-mail and alerting you when a contact sends a chat invitation. This behaviour can also be changed so that close really means close. Uncheck Allow this program to run in the background box in the Preferences tab.

Despite all of this, the ever-persistent Windows Messenger starts up again every time you launch Outlook Express or Outlook. To stop this happening in Outlook Express,

Tools

Options

Automatically log on to Windows Messenger

OK.

In Outlook,

Tools

Options

Other

Enable Instant Messaging in Microsoft Outlook

OK

If you'd rather not have Windows Messenger fire up with Windows, disable it here.

I keep getting hassled by a Messenger contact

No problem. Right-click the name in your contact list and select Block. You can still see when your contact comes online and you can unblock them at any time – or you can delete them from your contact list altogether. From their perspective, you now appear to be permanently offline, which means they cannot initiate a chat session. They can, however, still send e-mail to your Messenger e-mail address i.e. the one you used to register for a .NET Passport. For this reason, many people register a secondary, disposable e-mail address with Passport rather than their main address. In fact, a Hotmail address is as good an option as any, with the advantage that a ready-made Passport comes with it.

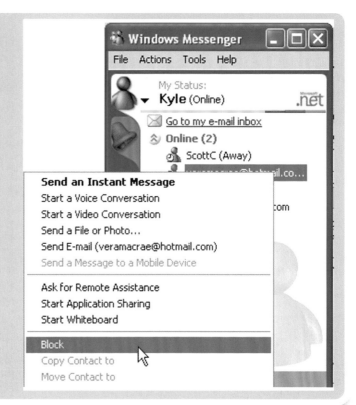

Can I use Windows Messenger to talk to contacts on other instant messaging networks, like AOL Instant Messenger or ICQ?

With the exception of MSN Messenger, which is compatible with Windows Messenger, the answer is no – or at least not at the time of writing. Seamless interoperability between instant messaging (IM) programs is one of the industry's bugbears. Unlike e-mail, where you can exchange messages with absolutely anybody who has an e-mail address, you can only chat to people who use the same service. The workaround is running several instant messenger programs simultaneously and maintaining separate lists of contacts.

Application sharing

Like NetMeeting before it, Windows Messenger lets colleagues share applications and collaborate on documents in real time. At its simplest, one user launches a program, opens a document and invites a contact to come onboard. The contact is then granted permission to edit the document.

Here we show two Windows Messenger contacts co-creating an image in Paint Shop Pro. The same principles apply with any shared application – a word processor, spreadsheet, database etc. – or, for that matter, a game. Note that only the contact who initiates the session needs to have the shared application installed on his computer. Note too that contacts must take it in turn to edit a document, and that the initiator can regain control of the application at any time.

1

(You)

Start Application Sharing

First, run Windows Messenger, check that your contact is online, launch the application that you wish to share and strike up a chat. The Application Sharing button should be visible in the right-hand window pane.

② (Your contact)

Accept

Your contact now receives the invitation and must click Accept to continue. If he declines, that's the end of the story.

③ (You)

Program

Share

Windows Messenger now displays a list of applications (including open Explorer and Internet Explorer windows) that may be shared. Select the appropriate option.

④ (You)

Allow control

Close

Click Allow control to enable your contact to access the application (don't click this if you want him to be able to see your application but not actively collaborate). Leave the two boxes below this button unchecked for now. Later, when you are familiar with how Application Sharing works, you might elect to check the Automatically accept requests for control box. This lets the second contact take control of the shared application on demand without first requiring your permission (see Step 6).

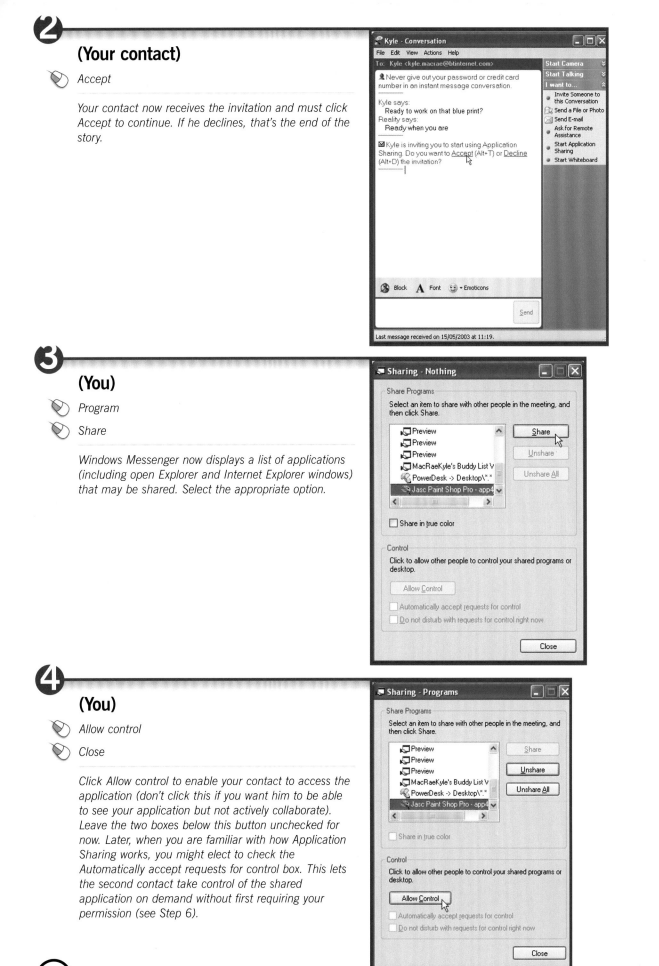

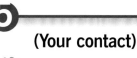

(Your contact)

 Control

 Request Control

*Your contact now sees the shared application in a
window just as it appears on your screen. To take
control – i.e. to use the program and contribute to an
open document – he must ask for permission. Note the
small floating window displays the connection status of
the session.*

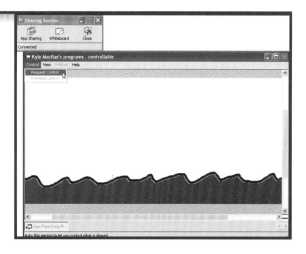

(You)

 Accept

*Click Accept and your contact can work freely with your
application and edit any open document (or indeed
open a fresh document). To regain control of the
application, click your mouse or press any key. If you hit
Escape, the second contact loses control immediately
and is also barred from requesting it again. This is an
emergency measure.*

(Your contact)

 Control

 Release control

*While he has control, your contact can work with the
shared application just as if he was sitting at your desk
(give or take a reduction in resolution, a slight jerkiness
and a short time-delay). To voluntarily relinquish
control, he uses the Control button on the window
toolbar.*

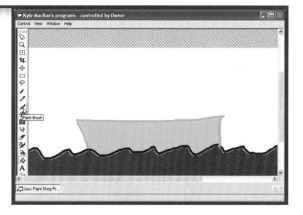

(Both)

 Close

*To end the Application Sharing session instantly, either
party may click Close on the floating window.
Remember to save the results of your collaboration.*

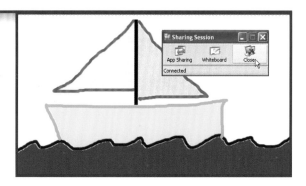

PART **Whiteboard**

Besides being able to share pretty much any application, Windows Messenger contacts can share a Whiteboard. This is basically a Windows Paint-style drawing board. The big difference with Application Sharing is that contacts can collaborate simultaneously on a Whiteboard document rather than having to alternate control.

Whiteboard is launched with a virtually identical procedure to that of Application Sharing: one contact initiates the session by clicking the Start Whiteboard button and the other reciprocates or refuses.

Use Whiteboard to collaborate on images over the internet with Windows Messenger contacts.

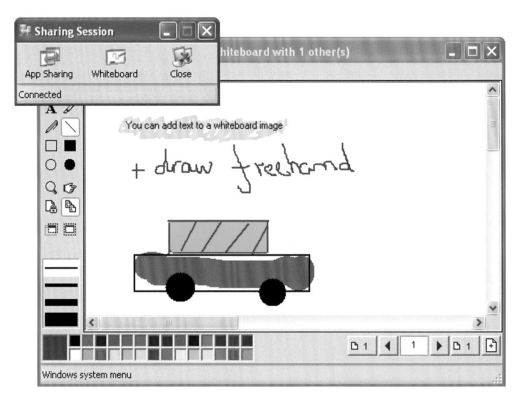

On the downside, you can only save a Whiteboard document as a special .NMW file, and not – as would be considerably more useful – an image. What's more, the first time you try to open a saved .NMW file, Windows XP installs a copy of NetMeeting, one of the precursors to Windows Messenger. This can be awkward and not in keeping with the Windows XP style.

Remote Assistance

With Windows XP's powerful Remote Assistance feature, you can invite another XP user to connect to your computer over the internet in order to troubleshoot problems. If you reckon this sounds suspiciously like the ultimate hacking utility, you would be half-right.

There are, however, two critical distinctions: a Remote Assistance session can only be initiated by the person seeking help (a 'Novice'), not a would-be intruder; and the whole system is protected with various permission-based safeguards and security measures. For one thing, optional but highly recommended password protection ensures that only the intended recipient of an invitation (an 'Expert') can make a successful connection. For another, an Expert has only the level of control that a Novice chooses to grant. At the start of a session, an invited Expert can see a Novice's Desktop but not do anything with it – hands-on control requires a further request and acknowledgement. Besides all of this, a Novice can end a session instantly and at any time by hitting the Escape key.

In full-control mode, an Expert can work with a Novice's computer just as if he was sitting at the same desk, up to and including modifying system settings, deleting files, fixing problems and wreaking havoc. In short, this feature has the potential to be extraordinarily powerful and must be handled with care.

Remote Assistance works much more smoothly with a broadband internet connection at both ends but is still functional with modems.

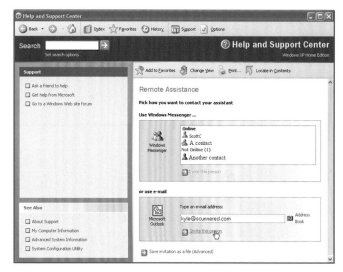

The Help and Support Center is one way to ask for Remote Assistance from a Windows Messenger contact or from anybody else via e-mail.

Getting connected

To initiate a Remote Assistance session, either invite a Windows Messenger contact or

 Start

 Help and Support

and look for the invitation link in the Ask for assistance section.

We will use the first method in the following worked example. The second option actually bypasses Windows Messenger altogether by firing off an e-mail invitation along with a file attachment that launches the Remote Assistance session. You do not need a .NET Passport in order to use Remote Assistance.

Here, we look at the procedure from both sides of the fence: a Novice called Steven and an Expert called (don't ask why) Reality.

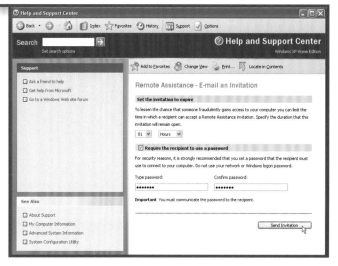

When inviting an Expert via e-mail, set a time limit for a response and use a password to ensure that only the intended recipient can connect. Do not, of course, include the password in the invitation e-mail.

Remote Assistance

Remote Assistance Invitation

From:	Kyle
Expires on:	20 May 2003 23:59:50
Password:	●●●●●●

If you do not know the password, contact Kyle.

Do you want to connect to Kyle's computer now?

    Yes   No

Kyle would lik

You can easily
instructions a

http://windows.m

Caution:

* Accept invit
* E-mail messe
* Before openi   ation
  at the above e

Personal message:
Help! I think I've broken something... again!!

When an Expert receives an e-mail request for assistance, he just clicks the link in the file attachment to initiate the session.

---

① (Novice)

Ask for Remote Assistance

First up, Steven the Novice must ask for help. He strikes up an instant messaging session with Reality the Expert and attempts to start a session. Remember, nobody can control your computer without your knowledge or permission, and Remote Assistance can only be initiated by the person seeking help, not offering it.

---

② (Expert)

Accept

The Expert now accepts or declines the invitation, whereupon the ball is shifted back to the Novice's court.

---

③ (Novice)

Yes

An important stage: Steven must now decide whether he really wants Reality to come onboard. This is the time to close all running programs and save open documents. When he clicks Yes, the Remote Assistance session begins.

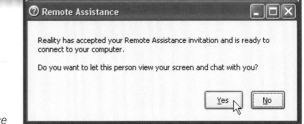

Remote Assistance

Reality has accepted your Remote Assistance invitation and is ready to connect to your computer.

Do you want to let this person view your screen and chat with you?

    Yes   No

(Expert)

Scale to Window or Actual Size

Things get a little spooky now. Reality can see Steven's entire Desktop display in a large window. That's all, mind: she can't actually do anything with it yet. This is called Screen View. If Steven has a wallpaper image on his Desktop, this is temporarily disabled to speed up the transfer of data.

At the top-right of the window are two buttons: Scale to Window and Actual Size. The first shrinks Steven's Desktop to fit the window, in which case some resolution and detail is lost; the second shows it in the full resolution of the original Desktop, in which case Reality may not be able to see the entire Desktop all at once and have to use scrollbars.

The left pane in the Remote Assistance window is a chat window that works just like Windows Messenger. It helps if both contacts close Windows Messenger now and continue their chat in this window. This is also the first opportunity that an e-mail-invited Expert has to talk directly to the novice. Just to reiterate: you do not need to use Windows Messenger or have a .NET Passport in order to use Remote Assistance.

(Novice)

From Steven's point of view, the only evident change is the new Messenger-like chat window. This is the time to tell Reality what the problem is. With a sound card, microphone and headphones or speakers at both ends, this conversation can be conducted over the internet just like a telephone call (see p132); otherwise, just use the chat window. Note the Disconnect button: at any time, Steven can click this to end the session and kill the connection.

(Expert)

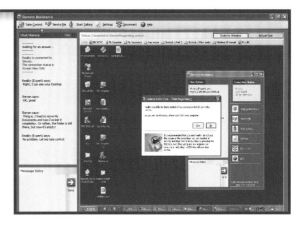

Take Control

Reality now clicks the Take Control button on the Remote Assistance toolbar. This generates a popup alert on Steven's screen.

7

(Novice)

 Yes

The important thing to remember – the really, really important thing – is that the Novice can kick the Expert out of the session at any point by hitting the Escape key. From here on in, Steven should limit his actions to typing in the chat window and not attempt to use the mouse.

8

(Expert)

As soon as the Novice clicks Yes, the Expert acquires full remote control over his computer. Reality can click Steven's Start button, launch Steven's programs, access Steven's files and folders, tweak Steven's system settings and in fact do absolutely anything that Steven himself could do. Spookier and spookier – especially for Steven, who now sits back and watches his mouse cursor darting around his screen launching windows and programs as if by magic.

9

(Both)

 Escape

To revert control of the computer back to the Novice, either player can press the Escape key. Reality can still see Steven's Desktop at this point – Screen View – but can no longer control it.

10

(Both)

Disconnect

To conclude the session completely, the Expert clicks the Disconnect button on the Remote Assistance toolbar or the Novice clicks the Disconnect button on the Remote Assistance chat window. Windows Messenger contacts can still communicate in a standard chat window but both the Screen View and Remote Control elements of the session are at an end – as too, hopefully, are Steven's problems.

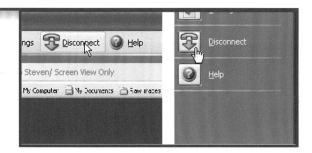

WINDOWS XP

Remote Desktop

Windows XP Professional (not Home Edition, sadly) comes with a similar, even more powerful tool called Remote Desktop. This lets you log on to your own computer with a User Account remotely across the internet. The effect is much the same as Remote Assistance – you get to work with your Desktop and applications exactly as if you were sitting at your desk – but there is no need for interaction with anybody else or, indeed, permission.

Log on to your XP Professional computer from anywhere in the world with Remote Desktop.

The benefits to a travelling worker are obvious, whether you log on from abroad to collect e-mail or from home to retrieve a file you left on your office-based computer. Configuration, however, is tricky unless the remote computer has an always-on internet connection and a static IP address. These conditions being met, here's what to do.

Setting up Remote Desktop

Remote Desktop requires a secure User Account so ensure that there is at least one account set up with password protection, be it your normal account or one set up specifically for this purpose. It can have either limited or Administrator status.

To enable Remote Desktop on the computer you wish to access remotely,

- *Start*
- *Control Panel*
- *System*
- *Remote tab*
- ⊙ *Allow users to connect remotely to this computer.*
- *Select Remote Users*
- ⌨ *the name of the User Account you intend to use to log on remotely*

Now configure the built-in Windows XP firewall to permit Remote Desktop connections.

- *Start*
- *My Network Places*
- *View Network Connections*
- *your internet connection icon*
- *Properties*
- *Advanced tab*
- *Settings*
- ⊙ *Remote Desktop*

If you use a third-party firewall, you will have to manually open the appropriate ports. Check the documentation or help menu for details.

Finally, make a note of the computer's current IP address (see Quick Q&A on p145) and log off your current session. The computer should be left online but paused at the Welcome screen with no user sessions in progress.

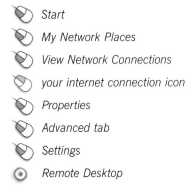

Remote Desktop will not work through a firewall unless you tweak the settings. With Windows XP's own firewall, this is straightforward.

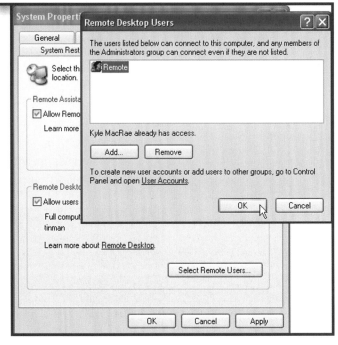

Stipulate which User Account(s) have permission to connect remotely. It might be worth setting up a special User Account for just this purpose (called Remote in this screenshot).

Getting connected

To connect remotely from anywhere across the internet, you need to run the Remote Desktop Connection client software. This is installed by default on both versions of Windows XP. To launch it,

- Start
- All Programs
- Accessories
- Communications
- Remote Desktop Connection

You can also install the client software on any other Windows-based computer from the XP installation CD-ROM (select Perform additional tasks followed by Set up Remote Desktop) or download it from www.microsoft.com/windowsxp/pro/downloads/rdclientdl.asp.

In the Computer: field, enter the IP address of the remote computer. When a successful connection is made, type in the appropriate User Account name and password.

If you plan to connect remotely on a regular basis, save the session settings as a file with the Save As button. In future, you can double-click the resulting file to initiate the session – but only if the remote computer still has the same IP address. As most ISPs allocate IP addresses dynamically, this may not be appropriate.

The remote computer's Desktop now appears in its native resolution on your screen but can be reduced in a scalable window. Either way, you now have immediate and unfettered control. When your work is done, log out as normal (p96) to close the session and return the remote computer to the Welcome screen.

Save Remote Desktop session settings as a file for one-click access next time around.

QUICK Q & A

How do I find my IP address?
The address you need here is your computer's public internet Protocol address i.e. a number that uniquely identifies your computer on the internet. This can be masked by hardware routers and it is not always easy to configure Remote Desktop to work with networks (for which read: see your System Administrator, if you have such a thing). However, if you have nothing more than a home network,

- click Start
- All Programs
- Accessories
- Command prompt
- TYPE ipconfig

Look for your internet connection and you should see the IP address listed. Here it happens to be 217.39.126.99. Alternatively, point your web browser at www.whatismyipaddress.com for instant results.

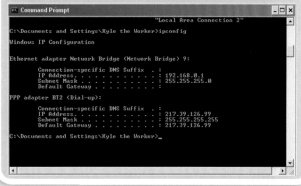

8

PART **8** WINDOWS XP
Appendices

PART 8 Appendix 1 Improving performance

Although Windows XP comes pre-configured to hit the ground running, it is perfectly amenable to user-customisation and fine-tuning. In particular, you can effectively 'turn off' the XP interface if a) you don't like it or b) your computer's hardware specification hovers near XP's minimum requirements (see p15). In the latter case, you can still enjoy the stability that Windows XP brings – no more crashes or memory faults – merely by compromising on a few resource-draining visual fripperies.

The infamous 'Blue Screen of Death' that indicates a critical, non-recoverable Windows error is a thing of the past with XP.

Prettiness vs. performance

Windows XP's funky graphical interface, Luna, comes at a price: all those drop-shadows, rounded edges, transparent icons and assorted eye candy require system resources. If performance is not all it could be, particularly if your video card is an older model, try selectively turning them off to see whether the resultant speed boost – if any – is worth it. For starters, you could lose your Desktop wallpaper, lower display resolution, reduce the colour depth and turn off the Windows sound scheme, all of which will make a marginal difference to performance.

However, Windows XP goes further and lets you trim all manner of superfluity.

- 🖱 *Start*
- 🖱 *My Computer in the Start menu*
- 🖱 *Properties*
- 🖱 *Advanced tab*
- 🖱 *Performance section*
- 🖱 *Settings*

Check the Custom option to enable or disable all manner of features: sliding Taskbar buttons, fading menus, pointer shadows and so on. Even Explorer's Tasks View pane can be nobbled here: uncheck Use common tasks in folders.

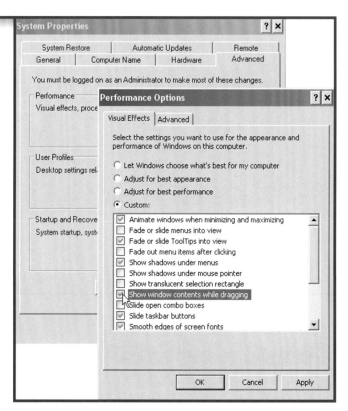

Selectively cut back on Luna's visual features with customised Performance Options.

For a one-hit approach,

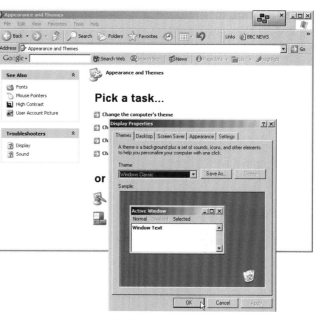

Turn back the clocks and fade to grey with a Windows Classic theme.

- ⊙ *Adjust for best performance option*
- 🖱 *Apply*
- 🖱 *OK*

This pares down Luna's interface to a minimum (but see the Quick Q&A box on ClearType first).

Alternatively,

- 🖱 *Appearance and Themes icon in Control Panel*
- 🖱 *Change the computer's theme*
- ⊙ *Windows Classic in the Themes tab*

At a stroke, XP looks like Windows 98. It may not be pretty but it can make a big difference in performance on a low-spec PC. Remember, it is still XP under the covers.

QUICK Q&A

What is ClearType?
ClearType is a little digital visual trickery that adds extra pixels to screen fonts. The effect is to 'smooth' fonts so that letters and numbers appear less jagged. However, ClearType is only intended for flat-screen TFT monitors and in our experience results are more impressive on small notebook screens than on desktop monitors. To experiment with ClearType, leave Smooth edges of screen fonts checked in the Performance Options window (see p148).

- 🖱 *Start*
- 🖱 *Control Panel*
- 🖱 *Appearance and Themes*
- 🖱 *Display*
- 🖱 *Appearance tab*
- 🖱 *Effects*

Try toggling between Standard and ClearType in the smooth screen fonts section to see which effect you prefer.

Background programs

- Start
- Help and Support
- Use Tools…
- System Configuration Utility
- Open System Configuration Utility

Or alternatively:

- Start
- Run
- msconfig
- OK

Why? Because this opens up one of Windows' best hidden tools.

Browse to the Startup tab and you'll find details of every program that starts automatically when you switch on your computer, including those that run idly in the background all day long, gnawing on RAM and slowing everything down. Such programs and processes often but not always lodge an icon in the Notification Area of the Taskbar, and you may be used to manually turning them off every time you restart. Here you can weed out the dead wood; just uncheck the box next to anything you would rather not have start automatically with Windows. When you restart your computer, as you must to make the changes effective, check the Don't show this message box on the popup warning, and then click OK.

For deeper pruning,

- Start
- Help and Support
- Use Tools…
- Advanced System Information
- View running services

Or alternatively:

- Start
- Run
- services.msc
- OK

This affords access to background activities that do not show up on the Taskbar or in the Notification Area, some of which are initiated by Windows, some of which are aspects of other programs, some of which are essential, and some of which are not.

Selectively turning off extraneous services can make a difference to performance but it is far from obvious which may safely be disabled. Rather than inventing the wheel here, may we point you to an excellent online resource on this subject: www.blackviper.com/WinXP/servicecfg.htm.

Tell Windows which programs and processes to load at startup, and which not to.

When you restart after tweaking Msconfig, you will see this confusing warning that seems to instruct you to undo your changes. Check the box and click OK to do away with it.

It's also worth looking in the Windows Startup folder for program shortcuts.

 Start

 All Programs

 Startup

Delete a shortcut to stop that program starting automatically with Windows. Conversely, you can drag any program icon to the Startup folder to have it launch automatically with Windows. The Startup folder's default location is C:\Documents and Settings\User Name\Start Menu\Programs\Startup.

Some programs reckon they have a right to start with Windows. Disabuse them of that notion here.

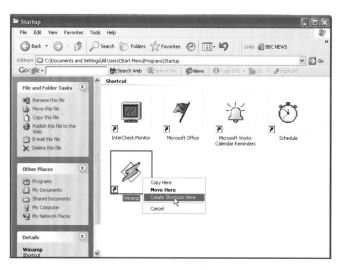

TweakUI

Microsoft produces but does not support a handy, free configuration utility called TweakUI (User Interface). This lets you fiddle with normally inaccessible or hard-to-find settings. For instance, you can bypass User Accounts passwords in the Logon section (see p101 for the long way around), customise system icons, turn off balloon tips (those intrusive Taskbar-generated bubbles), display or hide names on the Welcome screen and much, much more.

Download TweakUI here:
www.microsoft.com/windowsxp/pro/downloads/powertoys.asp

TweakUI is well worth the download and repays exploration and experimentation.

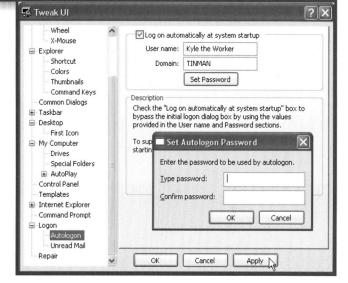

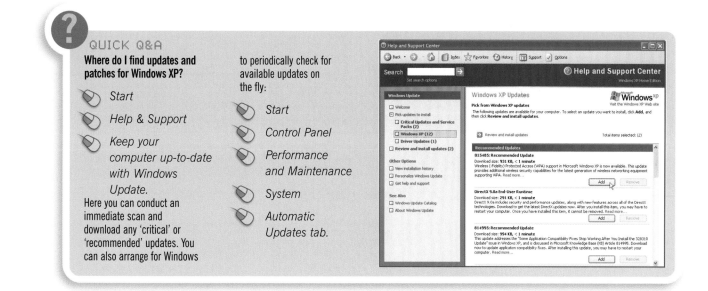

QUICK Q&A

Where do I find updates and patches for Windows XP?

 Start

 Help & Support

 Keep your computer up-to-date with Windows Update.

Here you can conduct an immediate scan and download any 'critical' or 'recommended' updates. You can also arrange for Windows

to periodically check for available updates on the fly:

 Start

 Control Panel

 Performance and Maintenance

 System

 Automatic Updates tab.

Appendix 2
Power management

Just a few words on power management. Although of course you can turn on your computer when you use it and off when you don't, or leave it running around the clock, where's the fun in that? There is plenty to tweak and play with in XP. We will assume here that your computer is ACPI-compliant (see the Quick Q & A box on p154).

Power Schemes

Power options are managed through a menu called, unsurprisingly, Power Options Properties.

Start

Control Panel

Performance and Maintenance

Power Options

The first tab deals with settings that govern the global behaviour of your computer. Click the drop-down menu in the Power Schemes section, make a choice and note how it affects the monitor and hard disk.

In Home Office/Desk mode, for instance, the monitor turns itself off after 20 minutes (adjustable) of inactivity. One nudge of the mouse or tap on the keyboard starts it up again.

You can also specify whether and when the hard disk should stop spinning. This saves a little electricity during idle periods and arguably reduces wear and tear on the drive but adds a momentary delay while the disk spins up again.

If you customise one of the standard schemes, click the Save As button and give it a new name (My Power Scheme, or whatever).

Turning off a CRT monitor when not in use saves a good deal of power but the benefit with an LCD monitor is marginal.

Standby and Hibernate

Standby and Hibernate are alternatives to turning off a computer completely, with important differences. When in Standby mode, the computer kills power to the monitor, drives and disks but ticks over in low-power mode, poised to spring back to full operation at any time. When in Hibernate mode, the computer turns itself off completely but Windows first saves the current contents of RAM to a file on the hard disk. This means that you do not have to close open programs or even save open files when hibernating; upon restart, the computer returns to precisely the same state in which you left it. Running programs are still running; open documents are still open.

You may have to enable the Hibernate feature on your computer first by checking the box in the Hibernate tab.

If your computer has a sleep button – not to be confused with the power and reset buttons – or if your keyboard has a sleep key that duplicates its function, you can configure it to activate either Standby or Hibernate.

Alternatively, or additionally, if your computer and keyboard lack a sleep option, you can use the main power button instead. Determine the function of these buttons in the Advanced tab.

What's more, if you select Shut down as an option for either the sleep or power buttons, you can turn off your computer quickly without going through the Start menu. However, this should be handled with care, as Windows XP does not acknowledge prompts from running programs ('Do you want to save this file now or lose it forever?') before killing the power.

If you can't be bothered or don't have time to close down your computer in an orderly manner, use the Hibernate feature to save your work.

Many keyboards have a special 'sleep' key that can be customised to activate Standby or Hibernate modes.

A sleep button can slip your computer straight into Standby or hibernation.

Closing down with the Start menu

Standby (or 'Stand By', as it appears here) is one of the options you see when you use the Start menu to close down:

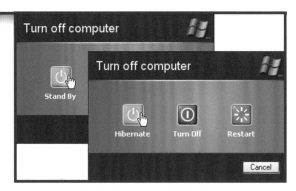

🖱 *Start*

🖱 *Turn Off Computer*

Hibernate is there too but curiously hidden by default; to toggle between the Stand By and Hibernate buttons, press the Shift key. If Hibernate fails to appear, go back and enable Hibernate in Power Options (see above).

Toggle between Standby and Hibernate with the Shift key.

Rise and shine

To rouse your computer from Standby or Hibernate modes, press the main power button. You may also be able to configure hardware devices like the mouse and keyboard to coax it back to action with a click or a tap of a key. A wake-enabled modem can restore the computer to full operation the moment it detects an incoming telephone call, which is obviously useful if you use your computer as an answering machine or voicemail system.

To check the status of your hardware,

🖱 *Start*

🖱 *Control Panel*

🖱 *Performance and Maintenance*

🖱 *System*

🖱 *Hardware tab*

🖱 *Device Manager*

🖱 *any listed devices*

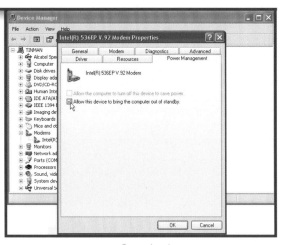

Some hardware can rouse a slumbering computer on demand.

If you see a Power Management tab in the Properties screen, check the Allow this computer to bring the computer out of standby. If there is no such tab, that device cannot be used. It's all a bit hit and miss, unfortunately.

In short, Hibernate mode is a useful time-saver if you need to leave your computer in a hurry (impending lightning strikes, panic call from the kids' nursery etc.); and Standby mode saves a little power while maintaining a state of readiness.

QUICK Q&A

What is ACPI?
Advanced Configuration and Power Interface is a hardware protocol that allows Windows to fully control the computer's power, unlike the earlier APM (Advanced Power Management) standard where power was managed by the system BIOS (Basic Input Output System). ACPI capability still depends on BIOS support, however, and Windows XP checks for this during installation. To check yourself, open Device Manager

🖱 *Start*

🖱 *Run*

⌨ *devmgmt.msc*

🖱 *OK*

and expand the System Devices list. There you should see an entry labelled Microsoft ACPI-Compliant System.

Appendix 3 The Registry and System Restore

The Windows Registry is a complex, multi-layered and essential repository of program and system settings that Windows draws upon almost constantly while running your computer. A problem here can have far-reaching consequences. However, any attempt to optimise, clean or fix the Registry is inherently dangerous, so make regular backups as you go along and always, but always, back it up before playing around with system settings. This way you can easily restore a 'good' copy of the Registry to get out of trouble.

System Restore

The easiest way to back up the Registry is with 'restore points'.

- Start
- All Programs
- Accessories
- System Tools
- System Restore

Now select Create a Restore Point and follow the wizard. Should anything go awry, you can revert to this safe point by running System Restore again and selecting Restore my computer to an earlier time. System Restore also saves a snapshot of other key system settings, including User Account details.

Windows XP runs System Restore in the background whenever it detects a new program installation and makes periodic routine restore points as you go along. However, if you prefer you can disable System Restore altogether: click the System Restore Settings link displayed in the first screen when the utility runs. This frees up a good deal of hard disk space and fractionally improves overall system performance. It also removes a valuable safeguard and is not at all recommended.

Get into the habit of making your own restore points before (not after) you install software, add new hardware or update drivers. These can prove invaluable if a recent change cobbles Windows. To make life even easier, download a smart little utility from Windows expert Doug Knox that creates a restore point at any time with a single click:
www.dougknox.com/xp/utils/xp_sysrestorepoint.htm.

Alternatively, see this article at the Microsoft Knowledge Base for instructions on how to back up the Registry without using System Restore:
http://support.microsoft.com/default.aspx?scid=kb;en-us;Q322756

Use System Restore to back up the Registry and safeguard other settings before experimenting with system-wide tweaks.

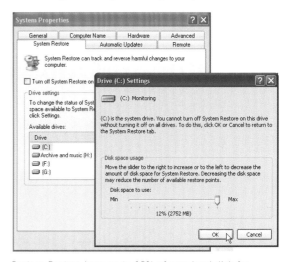

System Restore hogs up to 12% of your hard disk for restore points. You can reduce this or turn it off completely but we are strongly inclined to leave it be.

Tweaking the Registry

You can edit the Registry manually but this is a very bad idea indeed unless you know exactly what you are doing.

Here, though, is one neat tweak to whet your appetite. In Step 8 on p27, Windows XP prompts you for your name and organisation during installation. If you bought your computer with Windows XP pre-installed, there's a good chance that you are forever known as Crazee Computer Customer, or similar. To check,

My Computer

Properties

General tab and see what is listed there

To change your registration details,

Start

Run

regedit

OK

This launches the Registry Editor program. Now click on the plus sign next to HKEY_LOCAL_MACHINE in the left-hand pane to expand that particular branch of the Registry. Next, expand the Software, Microsoft and Windows NT branches in turn. Finally, click CurrentVersion and look in the right-hand pane for two entries called RegisteredOrganization and RegisteredOwner. Double-click each and change the Value data fields to suit.

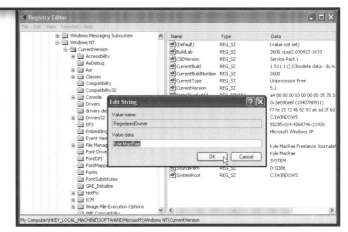

The Windows Registry is a database of everything that makes your computer tick. Back it up before making any significant changes – just in case.

Appendix 4
Troubleshooting

Most of the time, in the normal course of events, subject to circumstances and other vague qualifiers, Windows XP makes a pretty good job of starting normally time after time after time. This is in part helped by its reluctance to crash in the first place, and is further aided by various layers of self-protection. Nevertheless, you may occasionally find that Windows fails to start normally, or at all. What to do?

Advanced startup options

As Windows XP boots, press the F8 key. This interrupts the normal startup process and introduces the Windows Advanced Options menu. You may also see this or a very similar menu if Windows hangs during startup and you have to press the reset button.

One of the options here, as we have already mentioned, is Safe Mode. This loads a cut-down, stripped-to-the-bone version of Windows that lacks a great deal of functionality but lets you undo recent changes. If you need access to your local network when working in Safe Mode, select Safe Mode with Networking. The Command Prompt option is best left to those with a degree in DOS.

Should you install a new hardware device, update a device driver or install a new program and all of a sudden your computer crashes and/or refuses to work, restart it in Safe Mode and undo the changes.

If you suspect a driver problem, roll back to an earlier version if possible (see p160). To completely uninstall a troublesome device, use Device Manager. This can be accessed by

 *Start*

Control Panel

Performance and Maintenance

System

Hardware tab

Select the appropriate device, click the uninstall button on the toolbar, then power off the computer and physically remove the device. Try restarting.

To uninstall recent software, use the Add or Remove Programs utility, also found in the Control Panel.

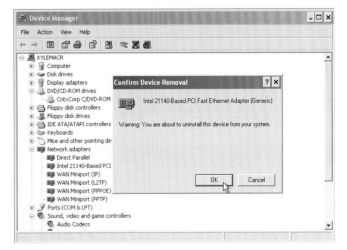

Safe Mode usually lets you restart your computer for diagnostic and repair work, with or without networking support.

Remove dodgy hardware with Device Manager in Safe Mode.

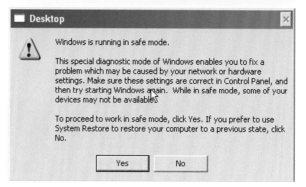

Safe Mode invites you to try System Restore. If manually removing hardware, rolling back drivers or uninstalling programs fail to work, give it a try.

Another Advanced Options alternative is Last Known Good Configuration. This undoes any recent changes to the Registry and restores it to the way it was last time you successfully started Windows. Unfortunately, this option is of limited value if you keep your computer running around the clock, as it could be days or conceivably weeks between restarts.

You can also use System Restore in Safe Mode. System Restore replaces the entire Registry with an earlier, working version.

Needless to say, it helps enormously if you remember to make manual checkpoints every time you make a significant change to your computer, such as installing a program or adding a hardware device. Do not rely on Windows alone (see p155).

A timely restore point can get you out of trouble.

Reinstalling Windows

If you cannot start the computer even in Safe Mode, you have two further options. One of these is to reinstall Windows over the top of your current version. This is not quite as drastic as it sounds because, barring unusual configurations, existing programs and files will be unaffected.

Boot from the Windows XP CD-ROM (see p18) and press Enter to run Setup. Ignore the Repair option for now; that comes next.

Setup begins as normal and asks you to accept the licence agreement. It then detects that you already have a copy of Windows installed and offers a repair option. Press R at this point. Setup now reinstalls the Windows XP operating system but leaves other files and folders alone.

In the best case scenario, this style of reinstallation cures Windows of ills and lets you carry on exactly as before. At worst, you may have to reinstall a couple of programs but your data should certainly be safe. As always, it pays to back up important files and folders regularly – before disaster strikes.

 QUICK Q&A

How do I close a 'hung' program without rebooting?
If a program stops responding to mouse or keyboard commands, use the Task Manager to close it. Press Ctrl + Alt + Del and look in the Applications tab. If a program is labelled Not Responding, highlight it and click End Task. This procedure is usually sufficient to allow Windows XP to recover gracefully from the problem without requiring a reboot.

To reinstall Windows, boot from the CD and press Enter.

Setup can reinstall Windows without affecting your existing programs, files and folders. Select the Repair option here. The alternative is a 'clean' install, in which case everything is lost.

The Recovery Console

Beyond starting in Safe Mode but short of reinstalling Windows lies the Recovery Console. This is the optimistically-named Repair option that we side-stepped a moment ago. Unfortunately, the Recovery Console is a text-only, graphics-free, command-driven environment that most Windows users will find unappealing and complex. Boot from the Windows XP CD-ROM and press R at the first screen. When prompted, select the copy of Windows that you intend to repair – usually there will be only one option here – and enter the Administrator account's password. Note that only 'the' Administrator can run the Recovery Console so refer back to p95-99.

At the C:\WINDOWS> prompt, type help and press Enter. This generates a list of possible commands. For instructions (after a fashion) on what each command can achieve, type help followed by a space followed by the command name, and hit Enter e.g. help chkdsk.

Among other things, and subject to certain restrictions, you can copy, rename and delete files, run chkdsk to repair the integrity of a hard dish, disable device drivers and mend the Master Boot Record. However, take the time to bone up on the Recovery Console before tackling any such tasks. For further details and instructions, see the Microsoft Knowledge Base article number 314058. (http://support.microsoft.com/?kbid=314058). A useful Microsoft multimedia presentation that covers Advanced Startup Options and the Recovery Console in some depth is also available on the web:
http://support.microsoft.com/default.aspx?scid=kb;en-us;324465

To start the Recovery Console from the Windows XP CD-ROM, type 1 at this prompt and press Enter. You will need the Administrator password to proceed.

The Recovery Console has no graphical interface but you can view instructions by typing help followed by a command name.

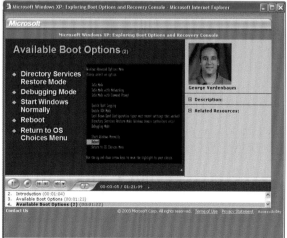

Get the low-down on boot options and the Recovery Console before diving in.

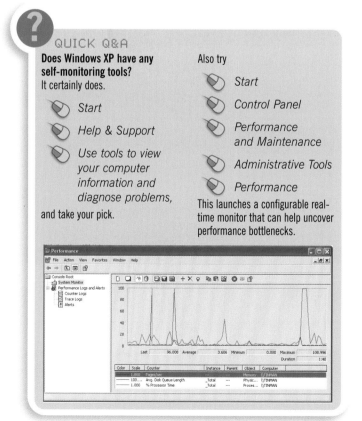

Appendix 5
Drivers

Hardware devices interact with Windows by means of instructions coded in software drivers. In virtually all cases, your hardware stands the best possible chance of working properly if it uses a driver specifically designed for Windows XP. That said, a Windows 2000 driver will sometimes suffice and you can always try Program Compatibility mode (p15) at a pinch.

When installing a new hardware device, the best bet – always – is to read the manual and use the software supplied. Windows provides an Add Hardware wizard in the Control Panel but it tells you the same thing. Only when you need to install a device for which you have no installation CD-ROM should you resort to the wizard.

When a manufacturer submits device drivers to Microsoft for verification and testing, and the drivers pass, they are granted a digital signature. This is a kind of quality guarantee; a digitally-signed driver should perform faultlessly and definitely not wreak havoc with other system settings. During driver installation, Windows XP checks for this signature and throws a wobbly if it fails to find one. Basically, you proceed at your own risk here – or ditch the device.

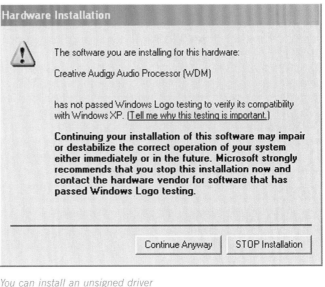

You can install an unsigned driver if you like but there is no guarantee it will work.

Rolling back a driver

Device Manager is home to driver details. Access it either through the Control Panel (click Performance and Maintenance, then System, and open the Hardware tab) or type devmgmt.msc at the Run command prompt.

Highlight any device and click the Properties toolbar button. In the popup window, look in the Driver tab and click Driver Details. If the drivers are signed, they are appended with a reassuring checkmark icon.

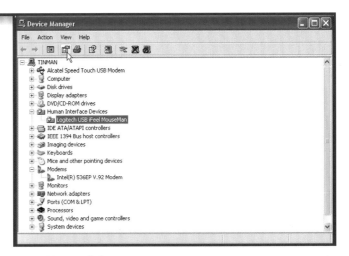

Device Manager is home to hardware. Here you can view driver details, update them, revert to earlier versions or uninstall devices completely.

Here you can also update a device driver: click the Update Driver button and follow the wizard. This is particularly handy when you have downloaded a driver update from a hardware manufacturer's website. Be sure to check Install from a list or specific location in the first screen, and browse to the saved file on your hard disk.

One very nice new feature in Windows XP is the Roll Back Driver button. When you update a driver, digitally signed or not, Windows retains a copy of the previous driver. It's a System Restore in miniature kind of thing: should the new driver not work, or conflict with other system operations, or stop your computer from starting, you can revert to the original driver without having to dig out or download old software. Log on in Safe Mode if that is the only way to start Windows.

Digitally signed drivers (left) have a special icon; unsigned drivers (right) carry a health warning.

If a new driver drives you nuts, roll back to an earlier version.

Updating a driver is easy with Driver Update.

WINDOWS XP

Index

ACKNOWLEDGEMENTS

The author and publisher would like to thank the Microsoft UK Press Team for their help in the preparation of this manual.

Author	**Kyle MacRae**
Project Manager	**Louise McIntyre**
Copy Editor	**Shena Deuchars**
Design	**Simon Larkin**
Page build	**James Robertson**
Index	**Nigel d'Auvergne**